THIRD EDITION

MORE READING POWER 3

TEACHER'S GUIDE
with ANSWER KEY

Linda Jeffries

Beatrice S. Mikulecky

PEARSON
Longman

More Reading Power 3 Teacher's Guide with Answer Key, Third Edition

Pearson Education, 10 Bank Street, White Plains, NY 10606

Staff credits: The people who made up the **More Reading Power 3 Teacher's Guide** team, representing editorial, production, design, and manufacturing, are Kim Casey, Dave Dickey, Amy McCormick, and Liza Pleva.

Text composition: TSI Graphics
Text font: Times

ISBN 10: 0-13-208905-X
ISBN 13: 978-0-13-208905-0

Printed in the United States of America

1 2 3 4 5 6 7 8 9 10 V036 17 16 15 14 13 12

CONTENTS

INTRODUCTION

More Reading Power 3, Third Edition is intended for intermediate-level students in high school, college, or adult education. Students who use this book are expected to have a vocabulary of about 800–1,000 words and be familiar with most tenses in English.

Research has shown that reading is a complex process in which the reader interacts with the text at various levels. For comprehension to take place, the reader needs to know what letters look like in English, how they form words, what the words mean, how they are used in sentences, and how ideas are expressed and organized in sentences, paragraphs, and longer pieces of writing.

To promote improvement successfully, a reading program needs to deal with all these aspects of reading. This is the multifaceted approach that is taken in *More Reading Power 3, Third Edition,* which aims to:

- Get students reading as much as possible.
- Help them become more fluent readers.
- Provide direct instruction in frequently used vocabulary.
- Teach strategies and a study method for independent vocabulary learning.
- Teach skills and strategies for both sentence-level and discourse-level comprehension.

> The four parts of the book promote these aims in different ways and are intended to complement each other. Thus, teachers should NOT use the book sequentially, as they would most other reading textbooks. Instead, they should **use all four parts regularly** (every week if possible) so that students will be working continuously on all aspects of reading and vocabulary learning.

This format of the book gives teachers great flexibility in adapting it to their courses and to students' needs. Furthermore, it allows teachers to develop a "well-balanced language course" as defined by I.S.P. Nation, in which "equal time is given to each of the four strands of meaning-focused input, meaning-focused output, language-focused learning, and fluency development."[1]

- *Meaning-focused input*
  Part 1: Extensive reading
  Part 3: Aspects of the comprehension skills exercises

- *Meaning-focused output*
  Throughout the book: Pair and small-group discussion activities
  Part 1: Written responses to reading
  Part 3: The formulation and outlining of ideas, other writing activities (in this Teacher's Guide).

- *Language-focused learning*
  Part 2: Work on vocabulary, reference and syntax, use of vocabulary notebooks and study cards
  Part 3: Focus on Vocabulary sections, scanning for key words, work identifying frequently used linguistic devices and textual structures

- *Fluency development*
  Part 1: Extensive reading
  Part 3: Work on scanning, previewing, making inferences, and skimming
  Part 4: Fluency practice with timed readings

---

[1] I.S.P. Nation, *Teaching ESL/EFL Reading and Writing* (New York: Routledge, 2009), 1.

Re-reading allows students to consolidate their understanding of the passage, their knowledge of the vocabulary, and their confidence in themselves as readers, so where possible, passages in the student book have been used more than once for different purposes.

At the end of this Teacher's Guide, a **Sample Syllabus** has been included to give some indication of how work on the different parts of the book can be distributed over a semester and to provide suggestions for using the book in various kinds of classes.

General Guidelines for Using *More Reading Power 3*

- Students should be required to work regularly **on all four parts of the book**. This will allow them to develop multiple aspects of reading and to expand their vocabulary.

- Teachers can make an enormous impact in the classroom by serving as **model readers** for students and showing their own **enthusiasm** for reading.

- Students need to be **actively engaged** in the lessons—intellectually and emotionally—in order to counter perceptions of reading as a boring translation task.

- Students should work **in pairs or small groups** and talk about their work whenever possible. This enhances language acquisition and helps them develop new thinking styles. (As with all group work, teachers will need to make sure that all students participate and benefit from working together.)

- Teachers should always focus on the **thinking processes** needed to complete the exercises, rather than on the answers themselves.

- Teachers should **explain the purpose** of each type of exercise before asking students to do one. This will lead to greater involvement and learning.

- **Confidence** in one's abilities is fundamental to reading improvement. Teachers need to be sensitive to problems that could undermine confidence and quick to reinforce gains.

- Two important factors in reading are the ability to discriminate among sounds in English and knowledge of sound/letter correspondences. Students can develop these by listening to **teachers reading aloud** while they follow in the text (but teachers should NOT ask students to read aloud).

- **Movement and gesture** should be encouraged in the classroom since it reinforces learning and helps counter the idea of reading as a passive activity.

References

The following sources offer more information and advice about the theory and practice of teaching reading in a second language:

Day, R. and Bamford, J. *Extensive Reading in the Second Language Classroom.* Cambridge University Press, 1998.

Day, R. and Bamford, J. *Extensive Reading Activities for Teaching Language.* Cambridge University Press, 2004.

Grabe, William. *Reading in a Second Language: Moving from Theory to Practice.* Cambridge University Press, 2009.

Koda, Keiko. *Insights into Second Language Reading.* Cambridge University Press, 2005.

Mikulecky, Beatrice S. *A Short Course in Teaching Reading Skills.* Pearson Education, 2010.

Nation, I.S.P. *Learning Vocabulary in Another Language.* Cambridge University Press, 2001.

Nation, I.S.P. *Teaching ESL/EFL Reading and Writing.* Cambridge University Press, 2009.

Schmitt, Norbert. *Vocabulary in Language Teaching.* Cambridge University Press, 2000.

Waring, Rob. "The Inescapable Case for Extensive Reading," in Ed. Andrezej Cirocki, *Extensive Reading in English Language Teaching.* Lincom Europa, 2009.

www.extensivereading.net
www.erfoundation.org
www.robwaring.org
www.lextutor.ca
groups.yahoo.com/group/ExtensiveReading/

INTRODUCTORY NOTES

As explained in the student book, extensive reading means **READING A LOT**. If students are reading graded readers (books written for language learners), they should read *many* of them over the semester. If they are reading books written for native speakers, they should read *several* whole books.

Benefits of Extensive Reading

Extensive reading is the first of the four parts of this book because of the vital role it can play in improving reading ability—both comprehension and fluency. Many reading experts believe, furthermore, that extensive reading can also benefit language learning in other ways, including an expanded and deeper knowledge of vocabulary and collocation, a better understanding of syntax, and better spelling (Grabe, Nation, Waring).

Furthermore, extensive reading can lead to greater fluency in speaking and writing (Waring 2009). The reason for this is simple: Lots of reading means lots of language input—more opportunities to see how words, phrases, and sentences are put together in English.

> *"To gain fluent control over the language, the learners must meet [lexical and syntactical items] in real contexts to see how they work together, to see how they fit together. In other words, learners must get a "sense" or "feeling" for how the language works. This sense of language can only come from meeting the language very often and by seeing it work in actual language use."* (Waring 2009)

As students become more comfortable with the language, they become more confident in their knowledge, which in turn allows them to feel freer to use it and to produce more natural-sounding language themselves. This will not be a surprise to anyone who has ever read extensively in another language and has experienced the way words and phrases in the second language begin popping into your mind spontaneously, the result of a mental shift into that language.

Extensive reading is particularly valuable in an academic context as a source of written language input, since students who intend to pursue studies in English have an urgent need to be familiar with written English.

The following quotations present the case for extensive reading in an academic context:

> *"The studies show that extensive reading benefits quality of language use, language knowledge, and general academic performance."* (Nation 2001)

> *"Extensive reading may play a role in developing the capacity for critical thinking so important for success in higher education."* (Day and Bamford 1998)

> *"There is now considerable evidence from many sources to demonstrate that reading extensively, when done consistently over a long period of time, leads to better reading comprehension as well as improved abilities in several other language areas . . . . . . for academic programs that expect students to develop reasonably advanced academic reading abilities, there is no escaping the simple fact that one learns to read by reading (and by reading a lot)."* (Grabe 2009)

Success with Extensive Reading

The following is a list of the characteristics of a successful extensive reading course component (adapted from Day and Bamford 1998). The first point, as Nation has pointed out, is fundamental. If students do not truly read "a lot" they are not reading extensively and they will not benefit in the ways mentioned earlier. The other characteristics—2 through 6—make it possible for students to read a lot.

1. Students need to read **a lot**.
2. They must be allowed to **choose their books** and read at their own pace.
3. The reading should be **easy** for them.
4. There should be **no testing** on students' reading, though they can be evaluated for commitment and progress.
5. Classroom activities should give students opportunities to **share** their reading experiences and thus stimulate further reading.
6. The **role of the teacher** is crucial in advising, encouraging, and monitoring students, as well as serving as a model reader.

The questionnaire in the introduction to Part 1 will help teachers get a sense of students' experience (or lack of it) as readers in their first language. This may help teachers gauge how students will react to extensive reading. If it seems likely that students will be skeptical about the value of reading a book on their own, intimidated by the idea, or reluctant to engage in this type of reading, it might be advisable to **start gradually**. The short story and the nonfiction passage in Unit 2 have been included to allow students and teachers to work together as they read and react to their reading.

However, for students who are particularly insecure or skeptical, this may not be enough. Teachers may want to find additional stories or nonfiction passages, with appropriate content and at the appropriate level, for students to read and discuss as a class, before they move on to reading whole readers or books on their own. Alternatively, rather than having the whole class read the same story or passage, groups of students can be given different stories and/ or passages that they read and that then become the focus of discussion and/or activities. The groups can then share their reactions/impressions/conclusions with other groups or with the whole class.

When doing extensive reading for the first time, teachers may feel some anxiety about how they will manage this component of the course, since students will all be reading different books. In fact, teachers must effectively relinquish some of their control over students' learning. But as research has shown, allowing students to have more control over their reading and, thus, their learning leads to greater responsibility, satisfaction, and confidence on the part of the students.

Indeed, teachers will find that the extensive reading component of a course can be tremendously rewarding. Apart from the improvement they may see in students' reading ability, language ability, and level of confidence, teachers can discover a great deal about their students from the books they choose and the reactions they experience to their reading. And then, quite simply, for teachers who love reading, it's always a pleasure to talk about reading and books.

Motivation

Before starting any extensive reading activities, teachers need to make sure that students are open to the idea of extensive reading. Since the only reading students will have done in classrooms is probably intensive (the close examination of a passage), the concept of extensive reading will probably be new to them. Furthermore, some students may come from cultures where reading is not highly valued and they may have little reading experience in their first language. For all these reasons, they may not take the extensive reading part of the course very seriously, and may even consider it a waste of their time.

Thus, teachers should take some time at the beginning of the course to **convince** students of the value of extensive reading for language learning. Here are some suggestions for ways to do this:

- Explain the rationale for extensive reading and list the benefits, preferably in a format that conveys academic authority.

- Provide quotations from linguistic authorities, such as those given earlier on page 1.

- If relevant, teachers can tell about their own experiences with reading and language learning. At the beginning of the year, students are curious about their teacher. Hearing about his or her experiences can help break the ice (and remind students that teachers have also been learners).

- Tell success stories about students who improved their command of English through extensive reading (and passed exams, progressed in their careers, etc.).

Once students are convinced of the value of extensive reading, at least in theory, teachers need to do everything possible to keep them interested and involved. The key to motivation, however, is giving students the **freedom to choose** their own books or graded readers.

Within any group of students, as teachers know well, there will be a wide range of personalities and interests. This becomes evident when they can choose books for themselves (especially if they have the ability and confidence to read books for native speakers). A few books may be popular with many students, but the choices usually include a wide variety of genres and titles—romance, adventure, horror, science fiction, fantasy, biography, crime, and so on.

The argument for allowing students to choose is expressed eloquently by Nancie Atwell in *The Reading Zone*. Though she is a teacher of American (L1) children in middle school (ages 11–13), her views about choice in extensive reading are relevant for adult second-language learners as well. She says:

> "*We understand that when particular [students] love particular books, reading is more likely to happen during the time we set aside for it. The only surefire way to induce a love of books is to invite students to select their own . . .*
>
> *Our students have shown us that opportunities to consider, select, and reconsider books make reading feel sensible and attractive to children right from the start—and that they will read more books than we ever dreamed possible and more challenging books than we ever dreamed of assigning to them.*"[1]

In order to keep students motivated and create the conditions for them to read a lot, the reading material must be **easy** for them. Some students have the mistaken idea that they will learn more from books with many unknown words, when in reality, they will probably make poor headway in such books, find them very tedious, and give up. In any case—and this is something teachers should explain to students—the reality is that less vocabulary learning takes place (not more) when there are too many new words in a text.

Finally, students should not be subjected to traditional comprehension **testing** on their extensive reading, as that will change the game altogether and kill their enjoyment of the books. However, teachers do need to monitor students' progress, as explained later in the notes for Unit 3. In an academic context, teachers may also need to **set requirements** for the minimum number of books or pages that students must read per week or per semester. Putting pressure on the students this way may be the only way to make them take the reading seriously and find time for it in their lousy schedules.

---

[1] Nancie Atwell, *The Reading Zone: How to Help Kids become Skillful, Passionate, Habitual, Critical Readers.* (Scholastic Teaching Resources, 2007).

A Community of Readers

A vital factor in the success of extensive reading is the extent to which the students **share** their reading experiences with their peers and participate in developing a community of readers in the classroom. Many kinds of activities can make this possible, including those listed in the Student Book, in this Teacher's Guide, and in the books listed as references. The **role of teachers** in this reading community is crucial. They need to set the tone with their enthusiasm and demonstrate their own love of reading by actually doing it in class in front of the students. But the key to developing a lively reading community in the classroom is by providing frequent opportunities for students to talk among themselves about their reading. As research has shown, this leads to improved motivation and performance in various ways:

- Students "infect one another with enthusiasm for reading."

- They suggest good extensive reading materials to one another and provide one another with material by sharing books.

- "Peers provide an audience with which students can share what they have read."[2]

GENERAL GUIDELINES FOR EXTENSIVE READING

- The atmosphere in the classroom must be **relaxed and trusting** so that students will not be afraid to take risks and reveal their personal reactions to their reading.

- Students must be allowed **maximum freedom** in choosing their books, pacing their reading, and expressing their opinions. This is truly the **key to success** with extensive reading.

- Teachers can suggest books they think students may enjoy, but should NOT be judgmental in any way about students' choices. In extensive reading, the quality of the prose matters far less than the amount of reading.

- Students should **not be tested** on their comprehension or on vocabulary in extensive reading books. In later lessons, however, teachers may use texts that students have read (the passages in Unit 2 or others) to create extra exercises to practice the skills or strategies introduced in Parts 2 and 3.

- **Listening while reading** can build phonological awareness, decoding skills (processing of the letters and words on the page) and fluency. Whenever possible, teachers (NOT students) can read aloud while students follow in the text.

- The **dramatization** of fables, stories, or other kinds of narratives can give students opportunities for movement and expression that will increase their involvement in the reading and reinforce their language learning.

For further information or advice about extensive reading, see the list of references on page v.

TEACHING NOTES

The material and activities presented here are divided into three units, but it is not necessary to complete these in a strictly sequential order. Teachers who wish to get started immediately with extensive reading in books can go straight to Unit 3: Books after introducing the concept of extensive reading and having students complete the Reading Questionnaire in Unit 1. Afterwards, they can go back and spend time in class on the activities in Units 1 and 2.

---

[2] George Jacobs and Patrick Gallo, "Reading Alone Together: Enhancing ER via Student-Student Cooperation in Second Language Instruction" (International Reading Association, February 2002); available from: http://www.readingonline.org/articles/art_index.asp?HREF=jacobs/index.html).

Alternatively, teachers can also make use of the activities in Unit 3 while students are reading the fiction or nonfiction passages in Unit 2, expressing their reactions, sharing views about their reading and so forth.

Teachers can also continue to draw on the activities in Unit 3 for evaluating students' reading as needed throughout the course. Some of the activities might become a regular feature (such as Reading Circles, Book Conferences, and Book Files), while others might be more sporadic.

Reading Questionnaire *(page 2)*

This questionnaire can be an effective starting point for discussion about reading with the class. Answering the questions will lead students to assess their own reading experiences and comparing their answers with those of other students will encourage them to reflect on the particular cultural or family influences that have affected their reading experiences and ability.

What Is Extensive Reading? *(page 3)*

As mentioned above in the Introduction to Part 1, it is essential for the success of extensive reading that students **understand what it is and how it can help them**. After students have read this page, teachers can add some of the arguments mentioned on page 3 in order to convince students of the value of extensive reading.

UNIT 1
New Vocabulary in Your Reading

In this unit, students learn to deal with unknown words in their extensive reading. If there are too many new words, students will have trouble understanding and will become discouraged. For this reason, it is very important for students to read at an **appropriate level**. (See Choosing Books for Extensive Reading on page 16 in the Student Book and page 8 in this Teacher's Guide).

When the material is at an appropriate level (not more than 2% unknown words per page), students can make use of the strategies for dealing with unknown words that are presented and practiced in this unit.

GENERAL GUIDELINES

- Students should **not look up every new word**. This would slow them down, interrupt the story, and take the enjoyment out of reading. Vocabulary work is important, but it should be kept separate from extensive reading sessions. Students should look up a word only if they cannot follow the story without it.

- Students should be encouraged to **skip over** words that are not essential to the story (for example, in a detailed description). The exercises in Unit 1 are intended to show students that they can understand a lot even when words are missing, but some students may need extra coaching to accept this idea.

- Teachers can also encourage students to try **guessing the general meaning** of new words. Though they may not be able to arrive at an exact meaning (or translation), they may understand enough to allow them to continue reading.

- Students may need guidance and encouragement to use these strategies. With practice, they will **gain confidence**, and be better able to decide which strategy to use and when.

Exercises 1 and 2 (pages 4–5)

Teachers should make sure that students follow the instructions for the exercises. In particular, students should NOT try to guess the missing words. The purpose of this exercise is to demonstrate to students that they can understand a lot from a text even when they do not know all the words. Even with words missing—or with unknown words—they will probably understand enough of the general meaning to keep reading. (This is true, however, only if there are not too many missing or unknown words close together.)

Exercises 3 and 4 (pages 6–7)

The purpose of these exercises is to demonstrate that it is often possible to get a good deal of information about a word from the words or sentences around it—the context. Thus, when students encounter a new word that they cannot skip over because it seems important to the passage, they should try to use the context to construct at least an approximate meaning. That may be enough for the first reading. On further encounters with the word, they may be able to construct a more precise meaning.

UNIT 2
Fiction and Nonfiction

In this unit, students read and discuss a story and a nonfiction passage. The aim of the reading steps introduced here is to give students a general procedure that they can use later for reading many kinds of passages.

As part of the procedure, for both fiction and nonfiction, students are asked to read each passage several times. In fact, research shows that **repeated readings** of a text can enhance the comprehension and retention of ideas and vocabulary. Teachers should encourage students to go back and reread each text or parts of them as many times as they want.

GENERAL GUIDELINES

- After students have had a chance to read each passage on their own, teachers can further reinforce comprehension and decoding skills by **reading it aloud** as students follow.

- Teachers should leave plenty of **time for discussion** of the questions in Step D (page 11), in pairs, small groups, or as a class. Note that in fiction especially, the answers to the questions may vary according to individual interpretations of the story.

- Teachers should **check the vocabulary** items that students choose to learn and make sure that they are indeed useful. If the chosen items are not frequently used words or phrases, students can be asked to justify their choices (link them to their needs or interests). This will help students internalize the criteria for selecting vocabulary to learn.

Fiction (page 8)

Teachers should make sure that students follow all the steps in Exercise 1, A–E (pages 8 to 11) for reading and talking about the story. They should continue to use these steps when reading and discussing their extensive-reading books.

The short story "Good Morning" includes some vocabulary that might not be familiar to students and which has been glossed. The glossed words are not frequent vocabulary items, so students should not write them in their vocabulary notebooks and they should not be asked to learn them.

Nonfiction *(page 11)*

As with fiction, it is important for students to follow all the steps in Exercise 2, A–E (pages 12 to 15) for reading and talking about the passage. Some students may think of nonfiction—and history in particular—as just a boring series of facts and dates. However, there is considerable human drama in history as well; discussion can make students sensitive to this aspect. Students should be encouraged to get involved in the drama described in this passage about the Navajo Code Talkers. They should also be encouraged to relate this story to what they know about native populations (in the United States or elsewhere), about World War II, and about war in general.

Additional Activities

- **More work with fiction or nonfiction**
  If teachers feel that students need to build up confidence in their ability to read and talk about fiction or nonfiction in English, they can introduce **another story or nonfiction passage** before moving on to books in Unit 3. It may be advisable to look in collections of stories for language learners, rather than for native speakers, for stories that are not too difficult.

  Rather than using one story with the whole class, you may help students develop autonomy by having them work in groups, each group with a different story. After the groups have read and discussed their stories, each student should meet with a student from another group and tell each other about the story they have read.

- **Alternative instructions for Step E (fiction or nonfiction)**
  After they have retold the story or passage with their partner, students can be asked to retell it as a class, with each pair contributing a few sentences to the whole story, going around the classroom until it is complete.

- **Student-centered text exploration (fiction)**
  Since different people focus on different aspects of a given text when they are listening or reading, students should be allowed to elaborate their reactions in a way that is meaningful to them. To help focus students' thinking, teachers can offer a series of questions that explore different aspects of the reading experience and elicit different kinds of reactions. The following are some examples of possible questions:

  1. What sort of places did you see as you were reading?
  2. Did you feel that you were there with the characters? Why?
  3. Did you feel that you became one of the characters? Explain.
  4. Did you have strong feelings about some part of the story? Why?
  5. What do you think is the moral (lesson) of the story?
  6. Did this story remind you of other stories you know? Which ones and why?
  7. Did any of the characters seem like people you know? Explain.
  8. Would your mother/father/son (etc.) like this story? If so, why?
  9. Do you know someone who would not like this story? If so, why not?
  10. Which was the best part of the story? Why?
  11. Were there any parts that you didn't like? Why?

Students can choose four or five questions that they feel will allow them to express their ideas and feelings about the book. The questions can be the focus of discussion with a partner, with the teacher, or with a group of students.[3]

The activities listed above for fiction can all be adapted for use with nonfiction.

---

[3] Adapted from Mario Rinvolucri, "How useful are comprehension questions?," *TESOL Voices*, no. 204 (September–October 2008).

Choosing Books for Extensive Reading *(page 16)*

Students need to have access to readers and books at an **appropriate level**. This is crucial for success with extensive reading. Students using *More Reading Power 3* may be ready to read "real" books for native speakers. If they are not sure, they could start with a book written for young adults or children. These tend to be somewhat easier than books for adults in terms of plot line and vocabulary, though they are not necessarily easy for language learners.

Less confident or proficient readers should be advised to start with graded readers at Level 3 or low-intermediate. As students gain confidence, they can move ahead to higher levels or to books written for native speakers. Some students have the mistaken belief that if they choose books that are difficult for them, with lots of unknown words, they will learn more vocabulary. The more likely result is that they will simply get discouraged and stop reading.

At this level, there can be big differences in students' reading ability, depending on their confidence and fluency. It is very important for teachers to make sure that each student starts with a reader or book that they can read without difficulty and without needing to consult a dictionary. There are several ways to judge if a book or reader is at an appropriate level.

- **Reading level tests.**
  Some publishers of graded readers (such as Penguin) have level tests available on their websites. Teachers can download and use these tests to determine their students' reading and vocabulary level, and thus, the suitable level of graded readers for their students.

- **Vocabulary size tests.**
  These tests can give teachers a quick idea of the extent of a student's vocabulary and connect that information with a suitable book level. Various kinds of texts (including those developed by Nation) are available on the Lextutor website: www.lextutor.ca. (This website provides a variety of valuable resources for teachers.)

- **The 2% rule of thumb.**
  This is the simplest and easiest way to determine if a given book is appropriate for a given student. As students are advised on page 19, they should find no more than about 2% unknown words per page in their extensive-reading books. More than 2% means the book may be difficult for that student; 2% or less means the book is easy enough.

  How to check:
  — Count the total number of words on an average page.
  — Count the number of unknown words on that page.
  — Calculate the percentage of unknown words. For example, on a page with 100 words, there should be no more than two unknown words; on a page with 250 words, there should be no more than five unknown words.

There may, of course, be exceptions to the 2% rule. Some students—especially those from language backgrounds close to English—may be good readers in their own language and may also be good at guessing the meaning of unfamiliar words in a text. If such a student really wants to read a book with more than 2% unknown words—though NOT because they think they ought to or because they think it will please the teacher— then the teacher may give a provisional approval. But if the student gets bogged down, he or she can be asked to put the book aside and read something easier, which they are usually glad to do at that point.

- Students **must be allowed to choose books that interest them**, though teachers can make suggestions about books they think will be of interest.

- A class **lending library** can be set up, preferably with more titles than students. The collection can be expanded by combining collections with other teachers. It is important for the collection to contain a wide range of levels, genres, and subject matter. Students can have surprisingly different tastes in reading.

- If there is a **school library** with a cooperative librarian, the collection can be located there. This makes it accessible outside of class time and to a larger number of students, and may also make possible additional funding to enlarge the collection.

- Many books and readers have an **audio** version. Listening to the audio while reading the book may make the book more enjoyable and enhances language learning. Wherever possible, teachers should try to acquire the audio versions for class and library collections and should encourage students to use them.

Activities for Stimulating Interest in Books

- Teachers can make a regular practice of reading aloud the opening chapters of readers/books that might appeal to students (at an accessible level). If multiple copies (or photocopies) are available, students can follow along. If not, this can become a listening exercise (and teachers should read slowly).

- The teacher can extract a sentence from the reader/book (the last sentence sometimes works well) and put it on the board. Students then talk in groups about what they think happened in the book to lead up to that sentence. They can read the book to find out how well they guessed.[4]

- Take several sentences (at least three, but not more than six) from the reader/book that convey important information about the plot and write them on the board, not in order. The students work in groups to try to put the sentences in order and imagine what happens.[4]

- Find a short passage in a reader/book that is exciting and important for the story, and eliminate some of the words. These words should be content words relating to the plot or characters, not function words. (This is not a language exercise.) Students work in groups to try to guess words for the blanks.[4]

Guidelines for Reading Your Books *(page 19)*

Teachers may want to give particular emphasis to the advice for students here about finding a **regular time and place** in their day for reading so that it can become part of their daily routine. Students should also get into the habit of carrying their books with them all the time so that whenever they have free time they can pull out a book and read.

Students should be discouraged from looking up vocabulary as they read through a story or book for the first time. Looking up a word should be a last resort for when they really cannot understand the story without it.

If students wish to follow up their extensive reading with vocabulary work, this may be allowed, but it should *not* become a required part of extensive reading. When students encounter words they want to learn, they can make a light pencil mark in the margin. Later, they can look up those words and write them in their vocabulary notebooks.

---

[4] Adapted from Robert Hill, "Opening Books, Starting Reading," *READ Magazine*, no. 2 (2011).

Learn to Read Faster *(page 19)*

The introduction to Part 4 of this book discusses the reasons why slow reading can be a serious handicap for students: Slow readers are likely to perform poorly on exams and in courses and they will have more difficulty understanding what they read (see pages 228–230 in the Student Book and page 45 in this Teacher's Guide).

Furthermore, slow reading feeds into a vicious cycle of reading without understanding or enjoyment, which leads to less reading, even slower reading, and so on. One way to try to turn this around to create a "virtuous" cycle is for students to improve their reading rate (learn to read faster) so that they can read more, with better comprehension and enjoyment, which will lead to more reading, even faster reading, and so on.

Extensive reading often leads to improvement in reading rate in itself. Simply put, the more students read, the faster they can recognize and process words, phrases, and sentences. However, teachers can also help students improve more quickly. As students are told in the Introduction to Part 4, reading rate is partly a matter of habit—your eyes are used to moving across the page in a certain way. If you want to speed up, you need to break old habits.

Finding Your Reading Rate *(page 20)*

After students have found their reading rate in their extensive-reading book, teachers should make sure they keep track of their reading rate and check on their progress regularly (about once a week). Students should expect to see a drop in their rate when they start a new book, but normally it will pick up again after a while (unless the new book is considerably more difficult than the earlier one).

When students have filled up the Extensive Reading Rate Progress Charts on page 21, teachers can make photocopies of the page for them.

Reading Sprints *(page 21)*

These sprints can be a fun and effective way to help students break the habit of word-by-word or line-by-line reading. The procedure may at first seem complicated, but it is actually quite straightforward. In any case, teachers should be sure to read through the instructions ahead of time and explain them carefully to students to avoid confusion during the sprints.

The aim of these sprints is to change the way students move their eyes across the page. This is not always easy. Many students become anxious during reading sprints because they feel that they are understanding very little of what they read. Their comprehension will drop, in fact, but this does not matter. It is more important for students to succeed in sprinting by making their eyes jump down the page. Teachers can tell students to "grab" what they can from the page as they go.

GUIDELINES FOR LEADING READING SPRINTS ············

- Students will quickly realize that in order to reach their goal during the sprints, they have to read selectively, as in skimming. (See the introduction to Unit 6, Part 3, on page 211.) Students will also realize that even when they are sprinting, they can indeed grasp some meaning from the text, probably enough to follow the story. Above all, after they have completed the last sprints and read again in an unpressured way, most students will discover that their reading speed is faster than before.

- Most students enjoy the novel challenge of trying to read faster and faster, and, when they compare their initial reading speed with their final reading speed, are pleasantly surprised at the results. Some of the more cautious students may not see much difference at first. They need to be reassured and gently encouraged to push themselves more. If they do not manage to reach their goal the first time around during the sprints, they should be given a second, or even a third, chance.

- If students have chosen their extensive-reading book according to the guidelines, it should be appropriate for work on rate improvement. However, before starting the sprints, teachers should doublecheck that the books are not too difficult.

- Teachers can schedule several rounds of sprints throughout the course. They can also encourage students to continue to do sprints on their own, as a way to spur further rate improvement.

Notes about Evaluating Extensive Reading

The sections "Discussing Your Books" (page 22) and "Writing about Your Books" (page 24) include several kinds of activities that can be used for evaluating progress in extensive reading.

Evaluation is an important aspect of an extensive reading program. First of all, for administrative reasons, teachers may need some tangible measure of students' progress in this part of the course. The fact that the teacher evaluates students' progress also reinforces the idea that extensive reading is an integral part of the course that must be taken seriously. Finally, these activities provide students with opportunities for sharing their reading experiences and for learning new ways of thinking, talking, and writing about books and ideas.

For the purposes of extensive reading, the criteria for evaluation should not be the accuracy of students' language output (pronunciation, grammar, or spelling), but their **commitment to and progress in reading their books**. Furthermore, though the activities presented on pages 22 to 24 can stimulate students, provide opportunities to use language, and provide data for evaluation, teachers must be careful not to overdo them. If students are too often required to follow up their reading with exercises, they may come to dread finishing a book.

Finally, and most important, teachers need to keep in mind the real purpose of extensive reading, which is to encourage students **to read as much as possible**. However valid a follow-up activity may be, it cannot replace the reading itself.

Additional Ways to Evaluate

- **Student-generated comprehension questions.** Students can be asked to write questions for themselves. They can then respond to these questions orally or in writing. This is best done after students have had a book conference and understand that the questions should not focus on details of the plot or characters, but should instead require them to elaborate in some way on their reaction to the book. (See the list of questions for Book Conferences on page 23.)

- **Negotiated evaluation.** One way to increase students' involvement and enhance their sense of responsibility is to allow them to choose how they want to be evaluated. Teachers can present a list of possible methods and ask each student to select one or two.

Discussing Your Books

Book Conferences *(page 23)*

Teachers may use the questions suggested on page 23 or others, such as the ones on the next page. In any case, students should be discouraged from retelling all the details of the plot. From students' answers, it is usually not difficult to tell if they have read the book and how well they have comprehended what they read.

Since these conferences are not tests but rather conversations about the books, teachers should not hesitate to help students express their ideas. The important thing is for students to gain confidence in their ability to communicate their reactions to their reading. Teachers should also feel free to contribute to the discussion with references to their own reading or experience, thus modeling how it is done for students.

Here are some suggestions for questions that can help students elaborate on their reactions to a book:

1. Expressive	Did you like the book? Why or why not?
2. Factual	Who is the main character? Where are the characters?
3. Summarizing	Can you tell the story in just a few sentences?
4. Sequential	What happened after that?
5. Predictive	What do you think will happen next?
6. Experiential	Has anything like that ever happened to you?
7. Critical	Do you think this could really happen?
8. Stylistic	Did the characters seem real?
9. Inferential	Why do you think the character did that?
10. Affective	How did you feel when you read that?

Reading Circles (*page 23*)

There are a number of different ways to organize the circles (groups). They can be established and maintained over the entire course so that the members of a group get to know each other well and become familiar with each other's interests, as seen through their reading. Alternatively, the groups can be changed from time to time, so that different students can get to know each other.

The circles should meet regularly (preferably every week) so that discussion of books becomes habitual for the students. While the reading circles are meeting, the teacher should circulate from one circle to another, listening to the discussion. The teacher may contribute a comment or react to students' comments with positive reinforcement.

Additional Activities for Reading Circles

- **Student-centered text exploration**
  If students spend too much time simply retelling the story, you can direct them towards more elaborative kinds of thinking by giving them questions like those in the **Student-centered text exploration** in this Teacher's Guide on page 7 (Part 1, Unit 2).

- **Short book talks**
  As a variation on regular meetings of reading circles, teachers can provide each group with topics relating to some aspect of their book. Each student should pick a topic.
  — Students have five minutes to think and plan what they can say about their book in relation to the topic (with notes if they wish).
  — Each student should talk in turn for two minutes about his or her topic. The student to the left of the speaker should time the speaker. The student to the right should ask a question afterwards.

Sample topics:

1. Describe a character in the book you are reading that interests you and talk about why you find him or her interesting. Does he or she remind you of someone? Do you identify with him or her?

2. Describe the setting (place and time) of the book you are reading. Is it important for the story? Is it interesting to you? Have you read other books with a similar setting?

3. What do you like best about the book you are reading so far: the characters, the setting, the plot, the style of writing, the humor, or some other aspect? Why do you like it?

4. Is there anything about the book you are reading that you do not like—the characters, the setting, the plot, the style of writing, or some other aspect? Why do you not like it?

5. Does the book you are reading remind you of any other books you have read or movies you have seen? If so, what does it remind you of and why?

6. Do you have strong feelings (positive or negative) about any part of the book you are reading? What part is it, what are your feelings, and why do you feel this way?

Book Presentations *(page 24)*

Before asking students to give presentations about their books, teachers should give one for the class that can serve as a model. The presentation should be short and personal, as per the guidelines for students. Above all, teachers should convey their enthusiasm for the book. Preferably, they should talk about a book that is at an accessible level for their students so that students who are inspired by the teacher's talk could read it.

To raise the interest level, teachers can talk about a book that has been made into a film that students might have seen. The talk can then be followed by discussion of the book/film.

GUIDELINES FOR ORGANIZING BOOK PRESENTATIONS

- Teachers should try to avoid scheduling more than four presentations per lesson so as not to lose the attention of the class. Early in the semester, students can be asked to sign up for a date with the teacher. This motivates students to finish their book by that date. In a course with enough class time, teachers can organize two rounds of presentations with each student presenting two different books, one at mid-term and one near the end.

- Students who might be fearful about talking in front of the class alone can pair up with another student. They can read the same book and then both can talk about it in front of the class, dividing up the questions and each giving their own opinion at the end.

- The book presentation should not be seen by students as a frightening ordeal, but as an opportunity to tell other students about their reading. If a student gets stuck while giving a talk, the teacher should not leave him or her to suffer, but help by supplying a word or asking a question.

- While students are giving their talks, teachers should encourage the rest of the class to listen quietly and attentively. To encourage students to pay attention, ask them to think of a question during the talk. Afterwards, the teacher can call on students to ask their questions.

- When a student has finished his or her talk, the other students should be encouraged to comment about the book or the speaker's opinion. Others who have read the same book can express their own opinions or reactions.

Writing about Your Books

Book Files *(page 24)*

If kept on file in the classroom, these cards can help students choose books to read. They can also help teachers keep track of which genres, authors, or books are most popular with their students.

Alternatively, the files can be virtual—created on a website dedicated to the course or to the program. In any case, they should always be available for students to consult.

Book Reports *(page 25)*

In these book reports, students should be encouraged to focus on their reactions to the book; they should not fill up the page retelling the plot. It can be helpful for teachers to show them a sample report (written by the teacher the first year, and thereafter by students) to serve as a model so they will know what is expected.

These reports should not be judged on their grammar, spelling, or vocabulary, but on the students' level of engagement with the book and the effort they make to express their reaction or opinion. Teachers can respond to the reports with brief written comments to create a dialogue focusing on the book, personal experiences, opinions, or other books they have read on related topics.

Students can be asked to keep their reports together in a binder or folder, which can become a kind of reading journal.

Reading Log *(page 26)*

This log is useful for both teachers and students as a way to keep track of the books read. For students, it can be a source of pride and satisfaction as the list grows.

Additional Extensive Reading Activities

- **Student-centered text exploration:** The activity that allows students to choose among a series of elaborative questions (described in the Teacher's Guide to Unit 2, on page 7, in relation to the fiction and nonfiction passages) can also be used with readers or books.

- **Reading aloud:** To entice students into reading books and give them some ideas about what they would enjoy reading themselves, teachers can read aloud the opening chapter(s) of a book, perhaps one a week, while students follow (on photocopies if there are not enough books available). In order to find out what happens, they must continue reading on their own.

- **Predictions about books:** One way to stimulate students to reflect on what they are reading and to use their imagination is to ask them to make predictions about the book when they are part way through. Students can write down their predictions for the teacher to collect; the teacher can hand them back after students have finished reading the book, so they can compare their predictions with the actual ending.

- **Reading survey:** Near the end of the course, students can be asked to take a survey of their classmates to find out which were their favorite books. Teachers can work with the whole class to develop the questions first. Then students can be asked to circulate and ask the questions, recording the answers. When students have completed the survey with their classmates, teachers can ask them to discuss the results, first in small groups, then with the whole class.

- **Further activities:** Relating to extensive reading can be found on the extensive-reading website and in the two books by Day and Bamford on the list of references on page v.

Suggested Reading *(page 27)*

The book list here includes only books written for native speakers, both for young adults and adults. Teachers who feel their students would do better by starting with graded readers can refer to the online catalogs of the publishers, including Cambridge University Press, Heinemann, Macmillan, Oxford University Press, and Pearson/Penguin.

All the books on the list are in print and available online at the time of publication, through the publishers or in bookstores in the United States and the United Kingdom. They may not all be available in bookstores in other countries, but can be ordered from the publishers or from many online bookstores (such as Amazon.com).

Teachers who wish to order books online internationally need to keep in mind the possible additional cost of customs duties. In some European countries for example, books ordered from the United States are subject to a steep customs fee, while those ordered from the United Kingdom are not subject to customs.

INTRODUCTORY NOTES

Research in second-language reading confirms what many teachers know by instinct and experience: vocabulary expansion is essential for improvement in reading ability. In *More Reading Power 3*, students will develop their vocabulary in three ways:

1. Through **direct instruction** of useful vocabulary.

   This is the main aim of the Focus on Vocabulary sections in Part 3. Teachers can do additional vocabulary work with words and phrases used in the four parts of the book. Most of the single vocabulary items are taken from the list of Frequently Used Words in English at the back of the student book, and therefore would be useful for students to learn. (However, the vocabulary items focused on in Unit 3: Guessing Meaning from Context are less frequent.)

2. By acquiring **the vocabulary-learning skills and strategies** necessary for them to become independent vocabulary learners.

   Direct instruction alone will not go far in helping students expand their vocabulary knowledge since there are inevitable limits to the amount of vocabulary that can be presented in any book or course. Given the constraints of scheduling, curriculum requirements, the need for exam preparation, and so on, the number of words or phrases that can be "taught" in a lesson, a week, or a semester is limited.

   Furthermore, according to research, long-term acquisition is possible only for learners after at least seven to ten encounters with a given word or phrase. In the light of this fact, teachers need to ask themselves, how many of the items they teach will students recognize or be able to use in six months' time?

   Thus, significant vocabulary development is only possible if students learn how to learn vocabulary on their own, so they can continue to make gains outside of and after the course. The approach to vocabulary learning presented in Part 2 aims to help students develop an effective study method that will ensure they
     a) select words or phrases to learn that will be useful for them, and
     b) encounter those words and phrases enough times to actually learn them.

3. Through **extensive reading**.

   As explained in the Teacher's Guide to Part 1, extensive reading (when it is truly extensive), gives students many more opportunities to encounter words or phrases and thus helps students consolidate and expand on what they learn in the classroom and through independent study.

   Furthermore, extensive reading provides students with vital input in how language is actually used and how words, phrases, and sentences are put together in a variety of contexts. Indeed, research has shown that extensive reading helps students acquire knowledge of collocation and usage, leading to greater fluency.

   To gain these benefits, however, teachers and students must take the extensive-reading component of the course seriously and students must do a considerable amount of reading—numerous readers or several books. A few stories or articles will not provide enough language input to make a difference. (See Teacher's Guide to Part 1.)

Which Language and Which Dictionary?

In the Note in the Introduction to Part 2 on page 32, students are advised to check with their teachers about which language they should use when looking up words and writing definitions. In Unit 1, they are also advised to find out which kind of dictionary they should use. Until recently it was believed that students should always use English to write definitions, and should use only English-language dictionaries when looking up words. Many experts, including Nation (2004), now believe this is not necessarily the most effective way for students to learn vocabulary. Intermediate-level students may learn vocabulary better with bilingual dictionaries and definitions in their own language because those definitions are more accessible and easier to remember.

Students who wish to use bilingual dictionaries should therefore be allowed to do so. They can be encouraged to consult monolingual-learner dictionaries in English as well, especially for some kinds of information, such as collocation, context, and variations in meaning because these dictionaries generally contain more information about usage than bilingual dictionaries.

Word List (Appendix)

In many of the exercises in Part 2 (as well as in the Focus on Vocabulary sections in Part 3), students are asked to refer to the Word List in Appendix 2. This list was compiled from the recently developed Pearson International Corpus of Academic English (PICAE), described below. It includes the first 3,000 most frequently used words in academic and general English.

For the purposes of this book, this list has several advantages over other word lists available at this time. First, it reflects current usage of the language, while the General Service List (GSL), one of those most commonly referred to, dates back to the 1950s. Furthermore, while the GSL was compiled from general, nonacademic sources, the PICAE word list was drawn largely from a corpus of academic texts. It includes most of the words common in general English, as well as the vocabulary needed by students who wish to advance their studies of English or to pursue an academic or professional career that requires knowledge of formal/academic English.

Another advantage of the PICAE word list is the extent and variety of the corpus it is based on, in contrast, for example, with the corpus used for the Academic Word List (AWL), often cited in EFL/ESL textbooks. That list was drawn from a rather small collection of academic publications in a limited number of fields, which makes it less suitable for students at the level for which *More Reading Power 3* is intended. The PICAE word list, on the other hand, is based on a variety of curricular and extra-curricular sources, including textbooks at the undergraduate level and student magazines, just to name a few.

Note that the words on this list do not each represent a whole "family" of words (as in the GSL and the AWL). Instead, forms are listed separately, and are only included if they are indeed among the most frequent words. This explains why the list is relatively long, 3,000 words, compared with the 2,000 words of the GSL. For example, the following are listed separately: *achieve, achievement; advantage, disadvantage; direct, direction, directive, directly,* and *director.*

The reasoning behind this choice was very simple: At this level, it may not be safe to assume that students will necessarily make connections among different forms of a word, especially if they have never before done any work on word segmentation. Furthermore, students will have a better idea of the usefulness of each form of a word and so can decide whether or not to learn forms that may be less frequent. Teachers should in any case help students become proficient in recognizing words belonging to the same family and can help them gradually expand their knowledge of word forms to include some that may not be listed. (See Part 2, Unit 4: Word Parts.)

PICAE, the Pearson International Corpus of Academic English

The frequency list was compiled from the Pearson International Corpus of Academic English (PICAE). It contains the top 3,000 words in the corpus ranked by average reduced frequency (to discount multiple occurrences of a word that occur close to each other in the same document).

PICAE comprises over 37 million words, including 13% from spoken and 87% from written material. As the corpus was designed to reflect material that the non-native speaker will encounter in academic settings where English is the main language used, PICAE includes both the English needed for academic work (72%)

(curricular English) and the English needed for various aspects of extracurricular life, e.g., dealing with university administration, reading student magazines (28%) *(extracurricular English)*. PICAE covers American, Australian, British, Canadian, and New Zealand English.

The curricular material includes a wide range of academic subjects covering the four main academic disciplines, namely the humanities, social science, natural and formal science, and professions and applied sciences. It also comprises lectures, seminars, textbooks, and journal articles at undergraduate as well as postgraduate levels. The extracurricular material includes university administrative material, university/student/alumni magazines, employment and career information, as well as TV and radio broadcasts.*

GUIDELINES FOR PART 2

- Teachers should work together with the **whole class** on the first exercise of each type (or the first item if there is only one exercise), checking students' understanding at each step and modeling the necessary thinking processes aloud.

- Whenever possible, teachers should ask students to **work in pairs**. That way, they can pool their knowledge of vocabulary. Talking about words also forces students to try to pronounce them, which reinforces memory (see the comments about pronunciation on page 18 of this Guide.)

- Students are encouraged to **choose the words they want to learn**. According to research, giving students responsibility for their learning in this way increases their involvement and motivation, making them more likely to actually learn the words.

- The tests in the **Test Booklet** for *More Reading Power 3* can be used either for evaluating students' acquisition of vocabulary or skills, or for additional practice or review.

- It is important for teachers to **assess** students' vocabulary learning. Teachers should keep up the pressure (in a friendly way) by checking notebooks and study cards often, and by testing frequently. See page 24 in this Guide or Part 2, Unit 2, Test 3 in the Test Booklet for a testing format that can be photocopied or simply copied onto a piece of paper.

- Students need to be encouraged to **review vocabulary** often and over a long period of time, so they will not forget words learned in past weeks or months. (See Studying Vocabulary, page 21 of this Guide.) To this end, teachers should periodically give students review tests.

- There are a number of useful **online resources** students can consult in addition to dictionaries. One of these is Check My Words at http://mws.ust.hk, which provides a variety of services, including information regarding spelling, forms, usage, and collocation, a system for storing and practicing vocabulary, along with personalized testing and word games.

TEACHING NOTES

UNIT 1
Making Good Use of the Dictionary

Choosing a Good Dictionary *(page 33)*

The dictionary used for the exercises in Part 2 is the *Longman Dictionary of American English* (2009) which is intended for low-intermediate/intermediate learners. The information about words given in this dictionary is typical of most learner dictionaries.

*The Pearson International Corpus of Academic English, Version 1, 2010 was developed and is owned by Language Testing, a trading division of Pearson Education Limited (http://www.pearsonpte.com/).

At this level, students should ideally have two dictionaries:

- **A monolingual-learner dictionary** intended for intermediate students. Learner dictionaries are preferable to other monolingual English dictionaries because they provide more information about how words are used. The definitions are also more accessible, since they are written with limited vocabulary and simple structures.

- **A bilingual dictionary**. These dictionaries provide accessible meanings for students, who may have difficulty understanding even the controlled language of learner dictionaries. Because bilingual dictionaries are bi-directional (English-to-first language and first language-to-English), they are also more helpful for productive use. One further advantage to the use of bilingual dictionaries is that it may be easier for students to remember definitions in their first language.

Pronunciation *(page 33)*

Pronunciation plays an important role in reading in two ways. If students cannot pronounce a word or phrase, they are much less likely to remember it. Many people have experienced this when reading a book written in another language, for example, a Russian novel. If you are not familiar with Russian, you may not be sure how to pronounce the names of characters and places and may have difficulty remembering them. Furthermore, learning to pronounce words (and listening to others try to pronounce them) involves another part of the brain, another learning dimension, which reinforces the memory of those words.

Research has also shown that knowledge of the way words sound in English helps students to decode them, that is, to process the letters and words on the page. The speed at which words are decoded greatly influences comprehension and fluency. In English, of course, pronunciation is particularly problematic since sound/letter correspondences can vary a great deal. For these reasons, teachers need to pay attention to pronunciation, even in a reading class. They should always pronounce new words for the class and give students practice saying them aloud.

Students also need to learn how to make use of the information about pronunciation that is available in dictionaries. Modern learner dictionaries use the symbols of the **international phonetic alphabet**, as in these exercises, but some dictionaries use other symbols. If necessary, teachers can use those symbols to develop exercises similar to the ones in Unit 1. It is not necessary for students to memorize the pronunciation symbols, since they can always refer to the examples in their dictionaries, but they will need practice recognizing the symbols and interpreting them.

Studies suggest that the first letters of a word are the most important in word recognition, so teachers should instruct students to **concentrate on the first letters**. Very often those first letters may be enough—along with other information from the context—for the reader to guess the rest of the word, and move ahead.

Additional Activities

- For more work on pronunciation, teachers can create additional exercises like the ones in this section. Where possible, the words should be ones students have encountered or are likely to encounter, that is, frequently-used words from the list in Appendix 2.

- Research in both L1 and L2 reading development suggests that instruction in **phonics** can also greatly help students with their reading. This can include teaching the most frequent and regular sound-spelling correspondences and practice sounding out words—saying aloud each of the sounds in the word and noting the spelling for each sound. Students should be encouraged to do this whenever they encounter a new word.

- For practice in **sound discrimination**, teachers can prepare sets of minimal pairs (*pin/pen, hot/hat, live/leave, it/hit, bath/bat,* etc.) and give students practice listening and identifying them correctly. (Lists of minimal pairs can be found online by typing "minimal pairs" into a search engine.)

Spelling (page 35)

Spelling is another kind of word knowledge that is important for reading. If students have only heard a word, but are unsure how it is spelled, they may not recognize it in their reading. Furthermore, knowledge of how words are spelled helps speed up students' decoding.

Students need to understand the importance of spelling in reading or they may not bother to focus on it. Teachers should, therefore, take the time to check students' knowledge of spelling during class. This should continue throughout the course. They should also require correct spelling on assignments and tests.

The more opportunities students have to think about sound-spelling correspondences, the more aware they will become of the **regularities in English spelling**. It is important for students to realize that regularities do indeed exist (especially with consonants) and that these can help learners acquire spelling for new words.

It is therefore useful to point out the regularities and to teach some of the old-fashioned rules, such as "*i* before *e*, except after *c*, or when sounded like /eɪ/ as in *neighbor* and *weigh*."

A number of websites contain useful explanations of spelling rules/regularities, including http://grammar.about.com, www.dyslexia.org, and www.riggsinst.org.

Parts of Speech (page 37)

In order to follow the syntax of a sentence, students need to understand the role of each word in the sentence. That is not possible unless they know what part of speech it is. Knowledge of the part of speech is therefore very important in constructing the meaning of a sentence.

Knowing the part of speech is also important because of the way it can help limit the possibilities in predicting what will come next in the sentence. Research has shown that prediction is a key aspect of the reading process. The more quickly and accurately students can make predictions and confirm them, the more fluently they will read. For example, if a particular word is an adjective, it is fairly likely that the next word will be a noun. (A prediction can be further narrowed down if students know anything about likely noun collocates for the adjective.)

Only one exercise has been included for determining part of speech, but others like it can easily be created.

Choosing the Best Definition (page 40)

Being able to choose the most appropriate meaning from among several in the dictionary is an important skill that can be developed with training. These exercises aim to raise students' awareness of the possible pitfalls of choosing one meaning from among several and give them practice in making choices.

As with parts of speech, teachers can easily create exercises that are similar to the one here, preferably with a learner dictionary, since they tend to include more examples.

The Way Words Are Used (page 43)

Last, but not least, students need to learn to make use of the collocational information and the example sentences in dictionary entries to get a fuller understanding of when a word is used and what other words are used with it. This aspect of word knowledge is essential, of course, for appropriate use of new words in speaking or writing. It is also important in reading, as knowledge about context and collocation can help a reader narrow down the possibilities of what may come next in a sentence, and so improve fluency.

When teachers focus on new words in reading passages, they should also provide information about usage—both collocational and syntactical. Students should then be encouraged to add notes about usage to their vocabulary notebooks. (Awareness of syntax and collocation will be developed further in Part 2, Unit 6.)

Focusing on words that students have already encountered in lessons or readings, teachers can create additional exercises of this type from the example phrases and sentences on a dictionary page.

UNIT 2
Learning New Vocabulary from Your Reading

Choosing Words and Phrases to Learn *(page 45)*

This unit trains students in an approach to new vocabulary that they can use for all their reading—in *More Reading Power 3* as well as in other books (though NOT in their extensive reading). A key feature of this approach is that students select the vocabulary that will be useful for them to learn. They then develop a personalized study method using vocabulary notebooks and word study cards.

Teaching students how to select the words to learn helps them avoid wasting time on words or phrases they may not need, and also makes them responsible for their learning, which increases their involvement and motivation and leads to more learning.

For the approach to succeed, students must understand the criteria behind choosing useful words. In fact, most students are relieved to have some way to focus their vocabulary learning, a task that may sometimes seem monumental to them. In the steps presented here, students will become familiar with the **Word List** in Appendix 2, on page 290 of the Student Book and also be asked to reflect on their own language needs. (For an explanation of the Word List, see the Introductory Notes to Part 2 on page 16 of this Teacher's Guide.)

Teachers will need to check students' work closely and ask them to justify the choices they make. They should also monitor carefully and often students' vocabulary notebooks and study cards to make sure students follow through after the initial class work.

Further practice in the process of selecting vocabulary to learn is provided in the Focus on Vocabulary sections at the end of each unit in Part 3. These sections also provide teachers with examples of exercise types for more vocabulary development. (See the lextutor website, developed by Tom Cobb at the Université du Québec à Montréal, for help in creating various kinds of vocabulary exercises: www.lextutor.ca)

With a few exceptions for key content words, the vocabulary in these passages and in most of *More Reading Power 3* is limited to the words on the Word List in Appendix 2—the first 3,000 most frequent words in the Pearson International Corpus of Academic English. (See page 16 in this Guide for more about the word list.) In further vocabulary work, it is advisable for teachers to continue to consult the list as one measure of the usefulness of any given word. As mentioned in the Student Book, other criteria may also be important, including relevance for a particular reading or for the students' courses, work, or personal interests.

If teachers wish to give students additional practice choosing words to learn, the passages they use should not be too difficult. Students will learn more from texts that contain some, but not too many, new words. If there are too many unknown words, they will have difficulty understanding the general ideas and will not be able to establish the context.

Note that in Exercise 5 students will be asked to look back at the vocabulary items they have written in the margins of Exercises 1 to 4 and to transfer them to their vocabulary notebooks, which will give them further opportunities to work with these words. Teachers may need to remind students that their notebook and study card entries should include the part of speech and the sentence where they found the word or phrase. It is important for this to become a regular habit.

- *Step 1* (**A** in the exercises): Reading all the way through the passage before focusing on new words or phrases allows students to get a general sense of the ideas and to establish a context.

- *Step 2* (**B** in the exercises): Research suggests that "re-reading" greatly enhances comprehension and so further builds context. Students may already have noticed words or phrases that are new to them; with this second reading and underlining, those words and phrases get more focused attention.

- At this point, teachers should check students' general comprehension of the passage, either through a short discussion or with simple questions that students can answer in pairs, such as the true/false questions in the Focus on Vocabulary sections in Part 3.

- *Steps 3 and 4* (**C** and **D** in the exercises): Students may understand the process better if teachers model their thinking aloud with a few vocabulary items in Exercise 1 on page 46. When students are working on Exercise 2, teachers can ask some of the more confident students to explain their choices to the class.

  Teachers should be sure to check the words and phrases that students have circled to make sure they are frequent and/or useful. At this point, students might not recognize phrases that are useful collocations, so teachers might want to point some out in the text (e.g., *depend on, index finger, aware of, flight reservation, concerned about, find their way around* in the text in Exercise 2). Even if students may be able to guess the meaning of a collocation, recognition will be speeded up by the fact that students have focused on it, written it down, and reviewed it. They are also more likely to acquire it for their productive vocabulary.

- *Step 5* (**E** in the exercises): Though students have had some guidance in Unit 1 on how to find phrases in the dictionary, this task may still present problems for some, and that may cause them to simply avoid looking up phrases. Teachers may want to provide further practice and assistance for those who seem to need it.

Studying Vocabulary *(page 50)*

To become independent vocabulary learners, students must develop a systematic method for studying vocabulary. This section introduces the use of a vocabulary notebook for collecting words to be learned and the use of word study cards for review. If students follow the recommended procedure for choosing vocabulary from their reading and then use vocabulary notebooks and study cards as suggested, they should encounter each item enough times to ensure learning, though that will need to be reinforced with subsequent reviewing and testing.

Reviewing is an important aspect of vocabulary learning that students may overlook when studying new vocabulary on their own. Even the most eager learners often move ahead continuously to new vocabulary and do not realize the importance of going back over words and phrases that they learned in previous weeks or months. Teachers should emphasize the need for regular reviewing—after each class, the next day, after a week, two weeks, or a month. The best way to encourage this kind of review is with frequent short quizzes of recently acquired vocabulary in students' notebooks, and regular review quizzes of vocabulary from earlier in the semester. (See About Individualized Testing of Vocabulary, page 23.)

Students must understand that "knowing" a word does not simply mean memorizing a dictionary definition. As they learned in Unit 1, there are many **different kinds of word knowledge**, and their vocabulary study should always include as much information as possible about a word or phrase, including pronunciation, spelling, part of speech, and different definitions.

All vocabulary work should also include information about **usage**, both collocational and syntactical. For that reason, teachers should present vocabulary in the context of a reading or a listening text, and vocabulary entries in notebooks and on study cards should always include the sentences where they were found.

Additional Vocabulary Activities

- **Vocabulary presentations**
  Students can be asked to choose two or three words or phrases that they have selected from their recent reading and give brief presentations in front of the class or a small group of students. In their presentations, they should write the necessary information for each word or phrase (the part of speech, the sentence where they found it) on the board, so that all the students can see it, and then dictate the definition slowly, so that students can write it down. They should also mention any relevant information about the usage.

- **Student-generated vocabulary exercises or tests**
  Asking students to create vocabulary exercises or tests for their classmates increases involvement and motivation, though teachers will need to make sure that the choice of vocabulary and the exercises are appropriate. Among the kinds of exercises that students could produce are:
  - Gapped sentences—If students write the sentences, teachers will need to check them. Otherwise, students can use sentences from dictionaries or other sources.
  - Gapped texts—These are best taken from a published source, not written by students. (See Exercise 4 on page 128 in the Student Book.)
  - Matching words or phrases and definitions (See Exercise 2 on page 143 of the Student Book.)
  - Word family charts (See Exercise 6 on page 130 of the Student Book.)

- **Word Maps**
  1. **Semantic or collocation maps**
     Students choose a key word from their reading and map out clusters of words and/or phrases relating to that key word as they appear in the text. The example below was created from the passage in Unit 2, Exercise 2 on page 47.

Teachers can create semantic maps together with students on the board. Or they can ask pairs of students to create maps. The groups and their placement can be according to grammatical categories, as above, or according to other criteria. Students can be asked to explain how each of the words or phrases relate to the key word in the middle. Alternatively, students can be asked to find as many ways as possible to put together the words and phrases in sentences.

2. **Word family maps**

   Teachers can easily improvise charts (like the ones in Exercise 6 on page 130 of the Student Book) or simple clusters with the different forms of words pulled from a reading text. Though students will learn more about these in Unit 4: Word Parts, teachers do not need to wait until students have done that unit to start work on word formation.

Vocabulary Notebooks *(page 50)*

For each vocabulary entry, teachers should require students to write all the information listed in the example (that is, word, part of speech, definition, and sentence in which they found the word). Students may be tempted not to bother to write some of the information, especially the sentence where they found the word, as it may seem time-consuming. Teachers can point out that it is this very fact—taking the time, making the effort—that increases the likelihood that students will remember the item.

Students do not have to write words in their notebook in the exact same format as the example. If they feel that another format works better, they can use that format. However, it is very useful to keep the word and meaning on separate but facing pages; this set-up enables students to cover one side and test themselves.

As for the order in which they write the words and phrases, students can personalize their notebooks in whatever way works best for them. Some students use small address or telephone books and write the words and phrases in alphabetical order. Others invent categories for the words and file them that way. Still others list the words and phrases according to where they found them.

Study Cards *(page 53)*

With their study cards, as with vocabulary learning in general, students should be encouraged to adapt them to their individual habits and learning styles. Some students, for example, use sticky notes instead of cards. They stick the words they want to learn that day or week around their desk at home or on a mirror or wall that they often look at, and then they remove the notes one by one as they learn each word.

About Individualized Testing of Vocabulary

Since each student will have different words in his or her notebook, teachers need to individualize vocabulary testing. This can be done with the photocopiable form on the next page or simply on lined paper. There are two ways to set up the quizzes:

- Students can write ten new words or phrases from their vocabulary notebooks onto the form. Then they should close their notebooks and write the meanings.

- Teachers can collect the notebooks, make lists for each student, give the quiz in the next class, and then return the notebooks.

Note that the second part of the vocabulary quiz form tests students on collocation. Teachers can ask for collocations for the same words as in Part A or different words, depending on what words/collocations students have encountered.

Name: _____ Date: _____

Vocabulary Quiz

A. **New words**   **Meanings**

1. _____ _____

2. _____ _____

3. _____ _____

4. _____ _____

5. _____ _____

6. _____ _____

7. _____ _____

8. _____ _____

9. _____ _____

10. _____ _____

B. **New words**   **Collocations including the words**

1. _____ _____

2. _____ _____

3. _____ _____

4. _____ _____

UNIT 3
Guessing Meaning from Context

This unit introduces the concept of context, and gives students instruction and practice in inferring meaning from context, first in sentences, and then in passages.

In recent years, some linguists and teachers have argued that teaching this skill is a waste of time, citing studies showing that learners may not be able to identify meaning after reading a word in context. There are several reasons, though, to doubt the conclusions drawn from those studies.

First, the studies often involved the reading of a single passage or story—not extensive reading as it is usually defined. Thus, students usually had only one encounter with each target word.

Second, the criteria for judging "knowledge" of vocabulary were very restricted: Subjects were asked to demonstrate their understanding of the meaning of target words by identifying synonyms or definitions. But according to some linguists, this narrow concept of vocabulary knowledge does not reflect the reality of language and vocabulary learning. As Nation (2001) says,

> *"Vocabulary learning is not an all-or-nothing piece of learning for any particular word. It is a gradual process of one meeting with a word adding to or strengthening the small amounts of knowledge gained about the word from previous encounters."*

Though a first encounter with a word (the only encounter by the subjects in the studies) may not give the reader enough information to formulate an exact meaning, it may provide some initial information about the word—a sense of what kind of word it is and when it is used—which later encounters will build on. In fact, while it may be true that context often cannot provide readers with precise meanings, it may help them begin the process of narrowing down the semantic possibilities for a word and of gathering information about usage and collocation.

Instruction on how to find context clues can help make students more aware of the kind of information that context can provide and how to extract it. With practice, students can become more efficient at this and more confident in their abilities. This, in turn, can help them become more fluent readers. When reading extensively, for example, students may often be able to gather enough meaning or information from the context to enable them to continue reading with understanding.

It should be noted here that **extensive reading** can play a key role in helping students become more confident about their ability to guess meaning. At the same time, the multiple encounters with words that occur through extensive meaning also allow students to expand and build on their knowledge about words.

As with each skill, teachers should explain the rationale behind learning how to infer meaning from context. It is also important to warn students of the limits to what can be inferred and the need to expand on their understanding in future encounters (and thus, the importance of extensive reading).

GENERAL GUIDELINES

- In all the exercises, students should try to write the general meaning of each word in English, however vague or circuitous, as this is excellent language and writing practice. If that is not possible for students, they may write equivalent words in their own language.

- Students who are inexperienced at inferring meaning may make wrong guesses at first, but they should be reassured that this is to be expected. It may help to advise them to read ahead of the unknown word to see if their guess fits in the larger context.

- Students may come up with answers to these exercises that are somewhat different from those in the Answer Key. Teachers should accept different answers as long as they make sense and students can justify them.

GUIDELINES FOR GUESSING MEANING FROM THE SENTENCE *(page 58)*

- Teachers should go through these steps with students before students do Practice 1. Then they should do the first item in the practice exercise together with the class, modeling aloud their own thinking as they look for contextual clues to arrive at the general meaning.

- Note that the target words in these exercises are not frequent vocabulary items and are not included on the Word List in Appendix 2. They should NOT be the focus of instruction or study unless the student has a particular need for or interest in a word. More frequent words were not used here as students might already be familiar with them and thus would not be able to practice guessing meaning. The choice of less frequent words also reflects the fact that students will be more likely to use this skill with less frequent words.

- In some of these exercises, students will need to make use not only of contextual clues, but also of their knowledge of the world in order to infer the meaning of the target words. For example, in Exercise 5, in order to understand the meaning of *cracks a book*, students need to take into consideration what they know about teenagers and the attitude of many teenagers towards books and learning.

- In the last set of exercises—Practice 2 and Exercises 7 and 8—the use of xxxxxx instead of the real word means that students cannot use information from the word to help them make a guess about the meaning. Though this may not reflect what actually happens when students read, it forces them to focus on the context, rather than simply make wild guesses from the spelling or the look of the word.

UNIT 4
Word Parts

This unit gives students practice in word segmentation. At the intermediate level, it is important for students to become aware of the way many words can be broken down into parts in English. Research has shown that recognizing and understanding word parts is a key step in developing decoding skills. The process of decoding is different from language to language. Students' ability to decode in English may be hindered by what they have learned in their native language, especially if that language is non-alphabetic or non-syllabic. These students in particular will benefit from focused learning about the syllabic structure of English words and the way they can acquire knowledge of prefixes and suffixes.

By learning how to analyze a word for its parts and becoming familiar with some common prefixes and suffixes, students will also acquire a useful strategy that will help them expand their vocabulary. Furthermore, recognizing suffixes and how they relate to syntax in English sentences is crucial for understanding sentence structure and following meaning. Finally, awareness of word formation patterns will allow students to develop new ways of processing words in English.

GENERAL GUIDELINES

- After finishing this unit, teachers should continue to work on word segmentation. They can ask students to analyze any suitable vocabulary item for its root, prefix and/or suffix, and then to try to come up with other members of the word family.

- When giving vocabulary tests, teachers can check students' retention of information about different forms of words they have studied by asking them to fill in a chart like the ones in Exercises 9 and 10.

Parts of Words *(page 68)*

These exercises are not intended to be used for pronunciation practice, and students should not be asked to produce the sounds of the words, especially since some of them are less frequent. However, hearing the words as they read them reinforces students' decoding skills, so teachers can read the words aloud as students look at them.

The information about Latin and Greek roots is intended to help students become more aware of relationships among words as well as among languages. However, it is not necessary for students to learn these roots. Learner dictionaries include this information.

Many of the words in these exercises are frequently used and are found on the Word List in Appendix 2. However, to give a range of examples of words containing the various word parts, it was sometimes necessary to include some words that are less frequent.

Partly for that reason, but above all, because the words in this unit are presented without any context, students should not be asked to try to learn the words presented in these exercises—unless they already are familiar with other words in the same family.

Word Families (page 77)

The forms that are given in these exercises and in the Answer Key are those found in the *Longman Dictionary of American English*, and are the ones most commonly used. Other dictionaries may include other forms, which may be acceptable as answers (if students can give proof of their existence). However, students should not be asked to learn infrequent forms.

UNIT 5

Collocations

This unit focuses on the way words in English tend to be used together in frequent combinations. This aspect of word knowledge has long been recognized as an important factor in fluency of language production.

What is perhaps less known is the role collocation plays in reading fluency. In fact, if readers are familiar with common collocations, they can process text more quickly because they can predict more often what will come next in the text. This means they can make fewer and more rapid fixations (when the eye focuses on a point in a text and sends visual input to the brain) and also fewer regressions (backward glances). The fewer fixations and regressions the reader makes, the faster and more fluent the reading.

GENERAL GUIDELINES

- Whenever a collocation comes up in class, teachers should point it out, explain its meaning and the context where it is used, and talk with students about how they would express the same thing in their native language(s).

- When possible, teachers should help students **analyze collocations** (especially idioms) to look for the semantic origins or some kind of logic that will help make them more understandable and/or memorable.
  Examples:
  heavy rain: Rain is water, and water becomes heavy if there's a lot of it, so heavy rain must mean a lot of rain.
  to sleep like a log: A log is a heavy object that cannot move, so this must be a very heavy, deep sleep.

- Students should be required to study collocations the same way that they study single vocabulary items, including them in their vocabulary notebook and on word study cards with the context where they were found. When testing vocabulary, teachers should also test collocational knowledge.

What Is a Collocation? (page 82)

The first aim of this unit is to raise students' awareness of how words combine in English and how that might be different from the way they combine in other languages. The unit also aims to help students realize the extent to which collocations are used by speakers and writers in

English. In fact, particularly as they deal with more sophisticated language, students will find that few sentences do not contain formulaic language of one kind or another.

One kind of collocation that is not included in the list on page 82 are conversational expressions, such as *See you later, What about you?, I can't believe it, That's too bad.* Teachers can point these out in the context of a dialogue in a story or during a listening exercise.

Learning Collocations *(page 83)*

To expand their knowledge of collocations, students need to begin making a conscious effort to include them in their vocabulary studying. The work in this unit can be a starting point in that direction, but only a starting point, since it is not possible in these pages to present more than a very small percentage of the thousands of frequent and useful collocations in English.

Because of the vastness of the task, however, it is unlikely that students will be able to acquire a very extensive knowledge of collocation through instruction and independent study. The only way they can significantly enhance their collocational knowledge is through massive language input—large amounts of language in real contexts—in other words, through extensive reading (and listening).

With collocations, as with single words, students will need to make a selection of those they want to learn, starting with the most common ones. Since there is no convenient list of frequent collocations to consult, they will need to check with their teachers at first and also learn how to find collocations in their dictionaries to find out if one is worth learning. For this, students are better off with a monolingual-learner dictionary, which usually includes more collocational information.

Exercises 1 to 4 introduce students to four different kinds of common collocations (phrasal verbs, adjective + noun, noun + preposition, and verb + noun). Teachers can point out other kinds of collocations as they come up.

Collocations in Academic Writing *(page 90)*

The collocations included in this section represent only a small percentage of those commonly used in academic writing and other formal writing, but will give students an idea of the ways that writers often combine words in these texts.

In Exercises 5 to 7, teachers can point out some of the additional collocations that are not listed on page 90 or in the boxes for Exercises 5 and 6. Alternatively, they can ask students to try to look for more collocations. (Examples: Exercise 5, 1. *have an effect on*, 2. *global economics*, 3. *results suggest*.)

Additional Activities

- Students can be asked to look for collocations (academic or otherwise) in other passages in *More Reading Power 3* or in other sources. They should then try to use their dictionaries to find out if the combinations they have chosen are indeed frequent and worth learning, but teachers will need to check their work and make sure students have made good choices.

- Teachers should point out that the academic collocations listed in the examples and Exercises 5 and 6 can be useful for writing assignments.

UNIT 6
Structure and Reference

In this unit, students develop their awareness of sentence structure and reference in English so that they will be able to follow meaning in sentences. Being able to grasp meaning quickly at the sentence level is a necessary skill for developing reading fluency.

Even at the intermediate level, teachers should not assume that students can do this easily. Their ability to parse sentences and understand relationships within a sentence depends a great deal on their language and instructional background. For some students, these exercises can serve as a quick review, but others may need additional practice.

Students will already have read the passages in Exercises 3 and 5 in earlier units. This will allow them to concentrate better on the syntactical features that are the focus of the exercises.

Teachers can give students further practice with sentence structure and reference by asking them to analyze passages in other parts of the book the same way they analyze the passages in these exercises.

Key Parts of Sentences *(page 93)*

The comprehension of any sentence depends on the reader's ability to identify its key structures, especially the subject and the verb. This ability may seem quite basic, but it should not be taken for granted, especially in students coming from languages with very different sentence structure.

Additional Activity

Nation suggests a useful way to work on sentence structure and meaning with an exercise that he calls **What does what?** Teachers provide students with a paragraph of several sentences and then ask students these questions: "What (or who) does what" or "What is what?" to identify the subject for each verb. Any passives in the original sentences must be made active, and any pronouns (such as *it, he, she, they, this*) must be replaced with the referent (*Teaching ESL/EFL Reading and Writing*, 2004, page 41).

Examples: (Sentences from Part 2, Unit 2, Exercises 1 and 3)

1. Which finger do you use to press a doorbell?
   What/Who — *you*
   does — *use*
   what? — *which finger . . . (to press a doorbell)*

2. People who are over 30 will almost certainly do it with their index finger.
   What/Who — *People who are over 30*
   does — *will . . . do*
   what? — *it   (with their index finger)*

3. More recently, the telegraph and then the telephone were also viewed as tools of linguistic destruction.
   What/Who — [people, scholars]
   does — *view*
   what? — *the telegraph and then the telephone (as tools . . .)*

Signal Words and Phrases *(page 95)*

Work on signal words and phrases here overlaps to some extent with work on signals for patterns of organization in Part 3, Unit 4. This is intentional, since these words and phrases play a key role in helping readers follow writers' ideas in writing in English, especially in academic writing. They often serve as markers to let readers know about logical shifts in the sentences or texts. Readers who do not notice signals or understand their functions may not be able to follow the ideas.

Teachers can ask students to identify signal words in other passages in the book (though only after students have read them for their original purpose) or in passages from other sources.

Work on identifying signal words and phrases in reading can tie in with practice in using these words and phrases in writing.

Additional Activity

Awareness of the role of signal words can be enhanced by looking at writing where they are used less, such as in news articles. The article in Part 3, Unit 1, Exercise 8, page 121 can serve as an example. Teachers can ask students to speculate on why this might be the case. All of the following are relevant:

1. News articles are written in a hurry.
2. They usually relate events, which are easier to follow than ideas, so signals are not necessary.
3. Readers often skim and skip large parts of articles, so journalists do not bother to make their writing coherent.
4. That is the conventional way of writing news articles.

Pronouns *(page 97)*

Students' ability to understand and use the various kinds of pronouns presented here will depend to a great extent on their native language. The aim in the exercises in this section is not to teach grammar, but to raise students' awareness of how referents are used in English sentences, so that they can more quickly identify them and arrive at meaning.

Teachers can give students more practice by asking them to analyze passages from other parts of the book that they have already read.

Synonyms and Related Words *(page 102)*

The ability to recognize synonyms and related words is yet another skill that will help students follow meaning in English, since writers in English frequently make use of them to avoid repetition.

Related words can include hyponyms, super-ordinates, antonyms, and words or phrases that are not normally considered synonymous or even related to a particular word, but can be interpreted as such in a particular context.

Additional Introductory Activity

Before doing Exercise 7, teachers can ask students to look again at paragraph 4 of the passage in Exercise 6 about the Tuaregs and find five phrases that refer in some way to the same aspect of the Tuaregs' lifestyle. The phrases are: *independent spirit, nomad way of life, come and go as they chose, move freely*, and *limit their travels and trade* (to express the opposite concept or antonym).

INTRODUCTORY NOTES

In *More Reading Power 3*, reading comprehension is viewed as a complex process that involves a variety of skills and strategies. These include "bottom up" decoding skills, such as recognizing letters and words, matching letters/words with sounds, and following syntax, as well as "top down" thinking skills, such as identifying topics and main ideas, connecting textual information with background knowledge, making inferences, and following the logic and development of ideas.

In Part 2, students worked mainly on text from the bottom up—at the level of words and sentences. In Part 3, they learn about and practice mainly (but not only) top down skills, those that are traditionally thought of as reading comprehension skills.

As in Part 2, it is essential for students to understand the skill or strategy that is targeted in each unit and how it relates to general reading ability. Raising students' awareness of their reading and thinking processes is the first step in their becoming more effective readers. Furthermore, if students are aware of the purpose of an activity, they are more likely to become involved in their work and less likely to feel that it is just busywork.

GENERAL GUIDELINES

- Each time a new exercise type is introduced, teachers should work together with the whole class and **model the thinking processes** aloud as they go through the exercise.

- Whenever possible, teachers should ask students to **work in pairs**. This requires them to talk about their work and so enhances meta-cognitive awareness. It also gives them opportunities for language practice. As always in a language classroom, teachers need to ensure that all students participate in and benefit from the activity.

- Many of the exercises in Part 3 lend themselves to **playful competition**. Adding the element of competition can increase the involvement of students and motivate them to take risks, but it should never be taken too seriously, as that might intimidate less confident students.

- In these exercises the actual answers are often less important than the way students get their answers. For this reason, teachers should **accept any reasonable answers** as long as students can justify them.

- Students should be encouraged to **defend their answers** when they differ from other students' answers or the Answer Key. This can help them externalize their thinking processes, and develop their productive language skills.

- Within each unit, students should work on the exercises **in order** since they become progressively more complex and difficult.

- Teachers may want to distribute exercises from a given unit across several lessons so as to **vary the type of activities**. That may mean that during a lesson students will work in more than one unit in Part 3.

- The exercises in Units 1 and 2 (Scanning, Previewing, and Making Inferences) work well as **warm-up activities** at the beginning of a lesson.

Focus on Vocabulary Sections

Each unit in Part 3 includes a Focus on Vocabulary (FOV) section that presents sixteen words or phrases in the context of a passage. All of the target words are drawn from the Word List in Appendix 2. The procedure for reading and selecting vocabulary is similar to the one in

Part 2, Unit 2. Students then work with the target words in various ways to ensure retention and expand their knowledge of usage, collocation, and related words.

But expanding students' vocabulary is only one of the aims of the FOV sections. Indeed, it could be argued that the 100 or so words that students learn from them may not be enough to make a real impact on their reading comprehension. By the time students work through these six sections, however, they should understand what it takes to acquire vocabulary and should each have consolidated an individual approach to vocabulary study.

The FOV sections can further serve as a blueprint for teachers to create additional materials for vocabulary development. This may be easier than some teachers realize with the help of online resources. One of the best is www.lextutor.ca (developed by Tom Cobb at the Université de Québec à Montréal), which provides teachers, students, and researchers with a variety of very useful tools for vocabulary work.

GENERAL GUIDELINES

- The placement of an FOV section after each comprehension skills unit was intended to help teachers organize vocabulary work at regular intervals, but the sections can be done separately from the units. Since some vocabulary is recycled in the passages and since the complexity of the readings increases, it would be advisable to work through the FOV sections in the order in which they are presented in the book.

- The reading texts in these sections can be reread for other purposes. For example, they can be used for further practice identifying key parts of sentences, pronouns, or synonyms and related words (Part 2, Unit 6), or for finding topics/main ideas of paragraphs (Part 3, Unit 5).

Additional Vocabulary Activities

See activities listed on page 22.

TEACHING NOTES

UNIT 1
Scanning and Previewing

Scanning (page 107)

Though scanning and skimming are often confused and are sometimes taught as the same thing, they are quite different skills. Skimming involves the processing of text for ideas, which requires complex thinking skills and for that reason, is the last unit in Part 3 of this book. Scanning, on the other hand, is a somewhat simpler skill that mainly involves a visual search for a specific item on a page, though it does require the reader to sort through the visual information to some extent.

Scanning for Information (page 107)

Apart from the fact that scanning is a useful skill in itself, one that we frequently use in daily life, another reason for asking students to practice scanning is to help them **develop flexibility** in their eye movements as they read. To complete the exercises and answer the scanning questions, students are forced to move their eyes very quickly around the page, which can help them break habits of reading word-by-word and line-by-line.

Scanning exercises also give students practice with word recognition and **visual processing**. When you scan a text for a certain piece of information, you have an image in mind of what you are looking for. It may be a certain kind of information (a date, a number, a name), or a specific word or phrase. As you scan, you try to match the image in your mind with something on the page. This kind of matching of expectations about a text with the visual information presented in the text is in fact a fundamental aspect of the reading process.

Finally, another reason why it can be useful to do scanning exercises in "authentic" material is to help students further **build confidence** in their ability to get information from text. Though some of the material in these exercises may contain quite a lot of difficult vocabulary, students will find that they do not need to know all the words in order to answer the questions.

Scanning for Key Words *(page 116)*

The concept of key words that is introduced here ties in with work that students will do later in Unit 3 on finding the topic of paragraphs since the key words are those related to the topic. Writers often repeat words related to the topic many times in order to help the reader follow the ideas.

Practice in scanning for key words can help students become more aware of how writers make use of key words as a cohesive strategy. It can also be useful for students when they are learning how to skim for the gist of a passage in Unit 6, since those words may help point the reader to the important ideas.

GENERAL GUIDELINES FOR SCANNING

- **Speed** is essential in these exercises. If the atmosphere in the class is sufficiently relaxed and positive, the teacher can use competition to motivate students. The exercises can be turned into a race, with either individuals or pairs competing.

- The actual answers to the exercises do not matter much, so teachers should not spend valuable time correcting or having students correct their answers.

- The scanning for information exercises give students an opportunity to write **further questions**, which can provide useful writing practice.

- These exercises can provide opportunities for **discussion**, since some of the cultural or other content may be unfamiliar to students.

- These exercises can serve well as warm-up activities, since students tend to enjoy the challenge of scanning against the clock and like the exposure to the various authentic materials.

- After students complete this unit, teachers can create other similar exercises. The texts can be authentic, since students do not need to read or know all the words. Scanning materials can also provide opportunities for discussion about cultural differences, personal experiences and preferences, and so on.

Previewing *(page 117)*

Previewing is a very useful skill that good readers often make use of. When introducing previewing, teachers can mention that we often preview in daily life. For example, we preview

- the newspaper by reading the headlines—to decide which articles to read.

- a letter by looking at the envelope—to decide whether to open it or throw it away (junk mail).

- a book by reading the front and back covers—to decide if it is interesting and whether to read it.

The benefits of previewing as a regular habit cannot be overstated. From a quick preview, the reader can:

- get a general idea of what the text is about;

- place it in a general context or within a mental framework;

- activate background knowledge about the subject;

- judge the difficulty of a text and calibrate the approach.

The reader is then a giant step ahead in the process of comprehending the text.

Practice in previewing also serves another purpose for students, and that is to help them gain confidence in their ability to extract information and ideas from a text without reading every word. In this sense, previewing is related to work on reading rate in Parts 1 and 4, and to skimming in Part 3, Unit 6. In fact, it really is a form of skimming, but compared with skimming, the aim of previewing is more limited. Readers preview for information about the title, author, subject area, genre, type of information, level of difficulty, and length; whereas when they skim, they are usually looking for the main ideas or gist, which requires more processing and comprehension of the text.

GUIDELINES FOR PREVIEWING LONGER PASSAGES

- As with other reading skills, before starting work on previewing, it is essential for teachers to explain the **rationale** (see page 117, and discuss the example on page 117 and the guidelines on page 120).

- In Exercises 6 and 7, students should use their **imagination** freely in making guesses about the texts and headlines. They may be able to guess more than they first realize.

- Throughout the course, teachers should require students to preview and check up on how effectively they do it, so that it becomes a **regular habit**.

- For more practice with previewing, teachers can use other passages from the book (including passages in the FOV sections, and in Part 4), or readings from other sources at a suitable level.

Additional Activities

- Working with a graded reader or short book that includes chapter headings, teachers write the headings in random order on the board and ask pairs of students to put them in the order in which they think they will occur in the text. Each pair should be asked to justify its ordering.

- Working with a nonfiction passage, teachers can give students a short list of topic-related words from a text they will read. Then students should try to predict as much as possible about the text, including the topic and the type of text.[1]

UNIT 2
Making Inferences

Good readers are in fact making inferences all the time when they read. One goal of this unit is to make students aware of what it means to make an inference and how it is an essential part of reading.

Another goal is to help students gain confidence in their ability to use all the information at their disposal—from the text as well as from their own store of knowledge—to make guesses

---

[1] Adapted from Robert Hill, "Opening Books, Starting Reading," *READ Magazine*, no. 2 (2011).

about meaning that is not explicitly stated, so that they will be more willing to depart from literal interpretations when they are reading.

Note that Exercise 6 introduces the concept of different text types, or **genres**, which will be explored further in Unit 5. In addition to simply identifying the genre, teachers can also ask students to identify aspects of content, language, and structure that are particular to that genre.

- Students should **work in pairs** on this unit so that they have to explain their answers to each other. In this way, they also can practice asking and answering clarification questions.

- There is **no single "right" answer** in many of these exercises. Any answer that a student can support with evidence may be considered acceptable.

- Teachers can **read aloud** the dialogues and excerpts from short stories in Exercises 1 to 4 as students follow in the book. However, students should not be asked to read aloud themselves until after the exercise has been completed and they have already heard the teacher read, and then not in front of the class, but in pairs.

- For further practice in making inferences, teachers can choose appropriate passages from stories or books, as in Exercises 1 to 4, or academic texts, as in Exercises 7 and 8. For further work on genre, teachers can create exercises like Exercise 6 with excerpts from other genres.

Additional Activities

- **Reconstructing the story from key sentences**
  This activity is similar to the first one listed under Previewing in Part 3, Unit 1 (Teacher's Guide page 33). Working with a short story that is not difficult, teachers take key sentences from the story and write them on the board in random order. In pairs or small groups, students try to imagine the plot and put the sentences into a logical order. Then they read the whole story and compare it with their guesses. (An alternative sentence order is not necessarily "wrong," since there may be other equally logical and possible ways for the plot to develop.)

- **Writing practice—sentences**
  To reinforce students' understanding of English syntax, teachers can require students to write the answers to the questions in Exercises 1 to 4 in clear and complete sentences. The better sentences can be put up on the board as models.

- **Writing practice—paragraphs**
  Students can also be asked to work in pairs and write another paragraph like the ones in Exercise 5 describing a job (without mentioning it, of course). These paragraphs can either be exchanged with those written by another pair of students who try to guess the job, or the teacher can select a few paragraphs to type up and print for the class.

UNIT 3
Understanding Paragraphs

Since discourse in English is usually topic-centered, identifying the topic is crucial to understanding English texts and work on topics is essential in a reading class. This unit begins by teaching students what a topic is, first with lists of words and then with paragraphs. Work on topics of reading passages will also help students better understand the importance of communicating the topic in their own writing.

Topics (page 147)

In these exercises, students work with simple lists of words so they can focus on the concept of topic and not be distracted by syntactic or other elements. These should not be confused with vocabulary exercises and students should not become overly concerned with the meaning of each word in the lists. It is usually not necessary for students to know the meanings of all the words, as long as they can identify the general word that is the topic.

This is also true for work students have already done in the units on guessing word meaning and making inferences. That is, if students understand that the topic is "parts of a car," they do not need to learn all the names of the parts (unless they are interested in auto mechanics). Similarly, in a paragraph or story, in order to follow the ideas or events, it may be enough to understand that an object is part of a car without necessarily knowing exactly which part.

GENERAL GUIDELINES

- Students should **work in pairs** so they can help each other with vocabulary and with the process of finding the topic. Talking together about the topic will also give them practice asking the kinds of questions that lead to comprehension.
- Teachers should encourage students to work **quickly** in order to develop efficiency in their processing of textual information.
- To reinforce their understanding of the relationship between the topic and the other words, students can be asked to make **diagrams** like the one in the example on page 151.
- Students should be encouraged to try to complete each exercise first without looking up words. They should be reminded that it may not be necessary to know the meaning of every word in order to find the topic.
- Since no context is provided for the words, students should not be asked to learn them from these exercises, unless they are already familiar with another word in the same family or they have a particular interest in or need for a word.

Additional Activity

Teachers can ask students to brainstorm in groups and come up with four topics (using the topics in the exercises as models). These topics can be written on the board. Pairs of students then select a topic and make a list of words that belong to it.

Topics of Paragraphs *(page 150)*

In languages other than English, paragraphs may not exist or may have a different function in the text. In English, paragraphs are important because they are closely tied to the ideas in the text. In order to follow those ideas, students need to have a clear understanding of what an English paragraph consists of and what its function is.

It may help students to understand these structural aspects of writing in English if they are aware of how they are similar to or different from the way writers organize ideas in their own language—in other words, of the **cultural differences** in communication.

For example, English-speaking people tend to prefer directness in both speaking and writing, which means they usually make their point (state their topic and main idea) at the beginning of their communication, and then they proceed to describe, explain, justify, etc. In other cultures, however, people present ideas in very different ways. They may, for example, give the description, explanation or justification first, and then make the main point at the end. Or they may never state the main point directly, but assume that the reader will infer it from the information in the text.

Another characteristic of writing in English is the fact that it does tend to follow a certain structure (and students will learn more about this in Unit 5). In other cultures, there may be less emphasis on the structure of a piece of writing, so readers may not be in the habit of noticing structural aspects—for example, looking for the topic near the beginning of a paragraph—and using them to arrive at the writer's ideas.

Note that there are, of course, exceptions to the general rules about structuring paragraphs and longer passages in English, particularly in news reporting and in less formal writing, such as emails or blogs on the Internet.

GENERAL GUIDELINES ....

- Teachers should point out that writers usually **repeat the topic** a number of times in a paragraph, and that this repetition can help readers follow the ideas. Teachers can remind students about the scanning for key words they did in Unit 2, and how this skill can now come in handy.

- **Graphic illustrations** like the diagram in the example on page 151 help students perceive the hierarchy of ideas in a paragraph in a very concrete way, with the topic literally positioned OVER the subordinate (supporting) facts and ideas. Requiring students to make diagrams in these exercises will reinforce the importance of topic and structure in English paragraphs. It will also prepare them for work on outlines in Units 4 and 5.

- Teachers may want to point out to students that in **different genres** the role and structure of paragraphs may be different. For example, in news reporting (in newspapers or on websites), paragraphs tend to be shorter and may not include a topic sentence. Students will learn more about these differences in Unit 5, but should be aware that at all levels, writing conventions may vary according to genre.

Main Ideas in Paragraphs *(page 156)*

As explained in the Student Book, the main idea is the writer's idea about the topic. It includes the topic and may be quite similar to the topic when the idea is simple and straightforward. But it is important for students to get into the habit of expressing the main idea in a complete sentence.

In some paragraphs, the main idea may be expressed in the **topic sentence**, that is, the sentence in which the topic is stated, usually at the beginning of a paragraph. However, this is not always the case, as the main idea quite often includes elements that are mentioned later in the paragraph. In the paragraph in Practice 4 on page 156, for example, none of the first three sentences contains the writer's idea about television, though each one contains part of it. An accurate and complete expression of the idea must include elements from each of those sentences (*television, families, effects, negative*), reformulated in a new sentence: *Television has negative effects on family life.*

This process of selecting and reformulating ideas—**summarizing**, in other words—is not easy for many students. Critical and synthetic thinking is required to select the ideas, and then students need to be able to find the appropriate words and structures in English to formulate them. But since this ability to summarize is crucial in an academic context, students need to begin acquiring the skill as soon as possible. Writing main idea sentences of paragraphs is one way to start. In Units 4 and 5, students will continue to practice writing main ideas and then move on to the overall idea of a longer passage.

When completing diagrams, students do not need to write complete sentences for the supporting facts and ideas. Using the examples and practice paragraphs as models, they can reduce those facts and ideas to words or phrases. This is excellent preparation for **note taking**, either from reading or lectures, when students will not have time or should not waste time writing out whole sentences.

- Teachers should always require students to write a **complete and correct sentence** for the main idea. It may help students to keep in mind the question: "What does the writer/ the paragraph say about the topic?"

- The main idea as well as the supporting facts and ideas that students write in their **diagrams may vary**. Teachers should make sure that the important facts and ideas are included, but can allow for differences in the way those facts and ideas are expressed.

- Though complete sentences are to be encouraged, teachers should keep in mind that the aim of the exercises is to improve reading comprehension, **not to teach grammar**. Teachers should not judge students' work on the basis of grammatical correctness.

- When underlining supporting facts and ideas in paragraphs (or when working on diagrams, outlines, or summaries), many students tend to be too inclusive. They need to be encouraged to be very **selective**.

- In these exercises, teachers should be sure to allow **time for discussion** about how students came up with their answers.

Following Ideas in Paragraphs *(page 160)*

The exercises in this section give students practice in following the language and the logic that writers use to express their ideas in English paragraphs. In each item, students are asked to predict how the last sentence will be competed. In order to do this correctly, they need to make use of various skills and strategies, including:

- applying logical patterns (analogy, categories, part-whole relationships);

- relating text to background knowledge of the world;

- understanding syntax (finding subjects and verbs; using verb tenses, negation, pronouns);

- extracting lexical information (synonyms, antonyms, hyponyms, collocations).

Whether or not students have had explicit practice with these skills (some are presented in Part 2, Units 5 and 6), they should be able to complete the exercises.

Teachers will come to a better understanding of the thinking processes involved if they complete several exercises themselves before introducing this unit to the students. Then they should take the time to go through the practice exercise carefully with the whole class.

Many students enjoy the challenge of trying to complete the linguistic and/or logical puzzles presented by these exercises. Teachers who wish to provide students with more exercises of this type will find some in the Test Booklet.

- Students should work **individually** in this part of the book. Once all students have completed an exercise, teachers can ask volunteers to read the items aloud and discuss the answers with the whole class.

- Though students should be allowed to work at their own speed in these exercises, they should be encouraged to **work quickly** so they will develop more efficient reading habits (and not translate every word).

- Students should be discouraged from using **dictionaries** while they are completing the items so that they develop their ability to deal quickly with unknown words by guessing a general meaning or simply skipping the word.

- After students have completed an exercise, they can go back and look up words they felt were important for comprehension.

Additional Activities

- **Concept Maps**

  Some students may grasp ideas and retain them better by making a concept map, in which ideas are set out on the page around the topic or main idea, rather than in the heirarchical format of an outline. (Grabe 2009)

- **Writing practice**

  Teachers can ask students to brainstorm in groups and come up with four topics. These topics can be written on the board (or the teacher can select some to write on the board). Then each student (or group of students) can select a topic, write a main idea, and then write a paragraph.

UNIT 4
Identifying the Pattern

About Patterns in Reading

The human brain can make sense of information better and remember it better if it is organized in some way. In fact, the brain does not work well with random pieces of information that must be stored as many separate items. It works more efficiently with information that has a recognizable order which relates to schema already present in the brain. This allows the brain to make sense of the information and to retrieve it later.

When reading, you can take advantage of this human preference for patterns. Good readers know that writers use patterns to organize their thoughts and express them, so they look for those patterns as they read. Since patterns in writing reflect ways of thinking, it is not surprising that writers in different languages tend to use different patterns. Thus, students who are learning to read in a new language need to learn how patterns are used in that language.

Research has shown that familiarity with the common patterns in English can greatly improve the ability of students to follow ideas in English text. As they move towards longer and more complex texts, it is important for them to get into the habit of thinking about the pattern and how it relates to the ideas.

In this unit, students will learn about five common patterns—Listing, Sequence, Comparison, Cause and Effect, and Problem-Solution—and the words that writers often use with each pattern to signal the main idea and the supporting facts and ideas. These patterns were chosen because students at this level are likely to encounter them and should not have difficulty identifying them. (Three more patterns are common in academic discourse: Description/classification, Definition, and Argument.)

The exercises here provide students with more practice outlining paragraphs. This can be taken a step further by including work with **graphic organizers**, as suggested by Grabe (2009). Instead of the hierarchical form of the classic outline, graphic organizers show the relationships among ideas in various ways. For example, for a paragraph with a sequence pattern, the supporting facts/ideas might be listed from left to right on a timeline. In a paragraph with a comparison pattern, there might be two large boxes, each filled with the facts/ideas of one of the two things being compared. Adding this visual dimension, according to Grabe, "is a powerful way to raise discourse-structure awareness." It also greatly enhances comprehension and reinforces memory, so it is an excellent study aid.

Teachers are advised to continue to ask students to identify patterns in later reading comprehension work. In a longer passage, a number of patterns may be involved since the overall pattern may be different from the patterns of some paragraphs.

Teachers should be sure to point out the **Note** after the boxes for signal words for the comparison and cause-effect patterns (on pages 180 and 183), which explains that writers sometimes combine signal words for one of these patterns with signal words for the Listing or Sequence patterns.

Example: Paragraph 1 of Exercise 5 on page 180
Comparison pattern signal words: *difference, However, while, on the other hand*
Listing pattern signal words: *One, Another*

GENERAL GUIDELINES

- As in Unit 3, students should be required to write **complete sentences** for the main ideas. The supporting facts and ideas can be expressed in more abbreviated form, with words or phrases (as in note-taking).

- When students are marking the facts and ideas in the paragraphs, and writing them in outlines, their work may vary to some extent. Teachers should accept their work as long as it includes the important facts or ideas, but not too many of the details.

- In a writing/reading class, teachers may want to point out to students that many of the signal words or phrases they meet here are also referred to as **transitions** or linking words in writing.

Additional Activities

- **Further practice**
  Teachers can use other passages in this book or in other materials if students need more work in identifying patterns, preferably paragraphs or short passages. As mentioned above, identifying patterns in longer passages may not be as straightforward.

- **Alternative introductory activity**
  The activity with numbers on page 172 can be supplemented or replaced by this activity with drawings:

  1. Show students the pictures below. They can be put on the board and covered until the class is ready for the activity, shown on a slide, or copied onto a separate page.

  2. Give students sixty seconds to study the pictures.

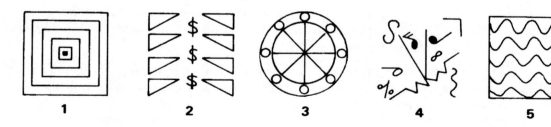

  3. Remove the pictures from sight and ask students to try to reproduce them from memory. (If students have photocopies, they may be able to see the pictures on the reverse side, so they will need to cover them.)

  4. Ask students: Which picture was the most difficult to remember? Why?

- **Student-generated graphic organizers**

  Rather than simply presenting models of **graphic organizers** to the class (as discussed on page 39), teachers can ask students to create models themselves for each pattern (after they have seen an example prepared by the teacher). The class can then choose which graphic organizer they think most effectively represents the relationships among the ideas in each pattern.

- **Writing practice**

  To give students more practice with each of the patterns, teachers can assign a topic for each one that fits clearly into the pattern and ask students to write a paragraph using at least three signal words or phrases.

UNIT **5**

Reading Longer Passages

In this unit, students learn how ideas are presented in longer passages in English, and they practice marking and outlining the important facts and ideas as ways to improve their comprehension and their retention of the material.

Additional Introductory Activity

In classes where most of the students have the same language background and the teacher is able to read in that language, a comparison of texts in English and the native language can enhance students' awareness of cultural/linguistic differences that may exist in the way ideas are presented in written texts. However, this activity is effective only if there are distinct differences in the way texts, and particularly news articles, are organized. (It has been successfully used, for example, in Italian university classes.)

1. Find two news articles about the same event, one in English and one in the students' native language. The English article should follow typical journalistic practice, using the "five Ws" and explaining the main facts about the event in the first paragraph. The other article should be written according to general journalistic practice in that language.
2. Give students a copy of the article in their language and ask them to discuss the following questions with a partner:
   a. What event is the article about?
   b. Where in the text do they find out the key facts about the event?
      (The answer to that will depend on the language. Teachers will need to think this activity through and, if necessary, do some research before trying it in class.)
3. Elicit answers from some pairs and discuss them as a class.
4. Give students the article in English and ask them to discuss the same questions with their partners. Elicit and discuss the answers, and underline the differences between the way the two articles present the facts.
5. Then ask students to look for other differences between the two articles. They should ask themselves:
   a. Which article is more formal in tone?
   b. Which one is more objective?
   c. Which one uses more direct quotation?
   d. How is the language different (more colorful, more descriptive, more ironic, more critical, more inferential)?

Reading for Study (page 195)

The skills that students develop here—text marking and outlining—are a continuation of the work they have done in Units 3 and 4.

Additional Activity

As in Unit 4 with patterns of organization, students can use **graphic organizers** to represent the relationships among the ideas and information in a more effective way than with simple outlining. Before asking students to create a graphic organizer, however, teachers should try it out themselves to make sure the passage is not overly complex and can be captured well with a graphic organizer.

Types of Passages *(page 198)*

The three types of passages presented here—news articles, feature articles, and textbook chapters or sections—have been chosen because students at this level often encounter these genres in their reading in English. Teachers may of course wish to introduce other types of text (genres), such as those included in Unit 2, Exercise 6, page 138. If so, teachers may wish to introduce the genre the same way the others are introduced in this unit, with notes about the structure (introduction, development, and conclusion) so that students can clearly see the similarities or differences.

Additional Activities

- **Cross-cultural/linguistic writing practice.**
  In classes that are linguistically and culturally homogeneous (for example, in EFL situations) and where the teacher is familiar with the students' native language, this activity can be a useful follow-up when students are learning about the structure of longer passages (page 194).

  1. Give students a news article in their own language, preferably an article that includes well-defined textual characteristics typical of that language and culture, and ask them (individually or in small groups) to rewrite the beginning of the article in English, following the rules for news writing in English, i.e., with key information in the first paragraph.

  2. To facilitate the task, teachers can provide some of the language students may need for the translation of key words or phrases. The focus of the task should not be on the accuracy of translation, but on the difference in the way ideas are presented.

  3. Depending on the languages/texts involved, teachers can also ask students about other aspects of text that might be different in the two texts, such as the level of formality, the level of subjectivity (for example, pronouns, author's presence), the use of direct or indirect quotation, and stylistic aspects (such as the use of colorful adjectives to dramatize a situation).

  4. Several of the better samples of writing can be put on the board and students can be asked to give their opinion about which is more "English" in structure and style.

- **Writing practice.**
  In a classroom with students from mixed language backgrounds, teachers can do an activity similar to the first one described above, all in English. The students can be given a news article in English (rewritten if necessary) so that the beginning does NOT follow conventional practice and ask students to rewrite it or reorganize it so that it is structured as expected in English.

UNIT 6
Skimming

As mentioned in the introduction to Unit 1, skimming is more complex and challenging compared with scanning. In scanning, readers usually need to recognize only the word or piece of information they are looking for. In skimming, however, they need to process more of the text, not just on a visual level, but also conceptually.

Research has confirmed that good readers frequently skim texts for the various purposes mentioned in the introduction to the unit on page 211. However, studies about skimming have not provided any clear answers to explain exactly how good readers actually skim—how they "get the gist" (the general ideas) from a text. Teachers can indicate where to find the important ideas—as in the Guidelines on page 212—but there will always be considerable variation, depending on the reader's purpose, knowledge and experience, and depending on the type of text.

The "normal reading"/skimming continuum[2]

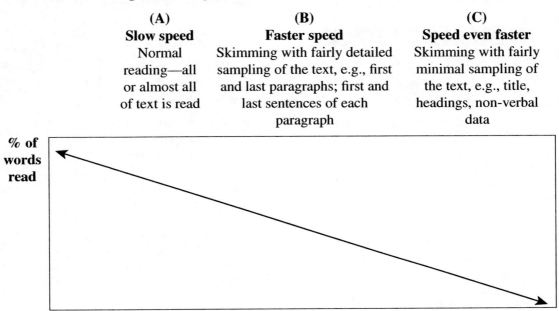

(A)	(B)	(C)
Slow speed	**Faster speed**	**Speed even faster**
Normal reading—all or almost all of text is read	Skimming with fairly detailed sampling of the text, e.g., first and last paragraphs; first and last sentences of each paragraph	Skimming with fairly minimal sampling of the text, e.g., title, headings, non-verbal data

% of words read

Basically, the reading process when skimming is the same as during "normal" reading, except that the reader samples (looks at and processes) less of the text. The relationship of skimming and reading can best be thought of as a continuum, as shown in the figure above.

Thus, as explained to students in the introduction to the unit, the key to skimming is *skipping* text. The difficult question, especially for language learners, is what parts of the text to read and what parts to skip. In fact, students can become good skimmers only if they already know how texts are structured in English and how writers in English use linguistic markers to signal the structure and ideas. That is why it is important to work with students first on topics, main ideas, patterns of organization, and structures of longer passages, and afterwards on skimming.

One of the difficulties of teaching skimming is the fact that no two texts are alike. Teachers can give students an indication of where they are *likely* to find the important ideas and information, as students should know already from their work in earlier units. But there is a great deal of variation among texts. Students cannot simply follow any rule when they skim; they need to be *flexible* in their thinking and *actively* look for the ideas. In fact, skimming requires great concentration.

Effective skimming also often requires the reader to make inferences. Because less of the text is sampled than in normal reading, there are inevitably large gaps in meaning that must be filled by inferring information and ideas from the sampled text.

---

[2] J.M.H. Rodgers, "Demythologising Skimming: the Operationalisation, Teaching and Practice of Skimming in a Second Language, with Special Reference to the IELTS Test" (Ph.D. diss., University of London, 2009).

The Guidelines for Skimming on page 212 provides students with a series of steps that will help them find important ideas when they skim. Teachers should go through these carefully, but as explained above, these steps are necessarily only an indication. Little is known about the process of skimming—how and why a reader chooses particular bits of text—but it does seem to vary considerably from reader to reader. This is why the Student Book does not include an example of text as it should be skimmed.

The only way students can develop an understanding of what it means to skim is by doing it. As with most other skills, continuing practice is the key to building competence and confidence. Students' ability to skim is closely related to their reading rate: Good readers usually can become good at skimming. At the same time, practice in skimming can help students improve their reading rate.

GUIDELINES FOR WORK ON SKIMMING

- Because skimming is such a complex skill and there are no agreed-upon rules, it is especially important for teachers to serve as **model readers** and explain to students their own thinking as they skim a particular passage.

- In Part B of each exercise students **time their skimming** of the passages. This is intended to encourage students to push themselves to look through the passages more quickly. At the same time, it allows for variation from one student to another, which is not possible when a time limit is set for the whole class (as commonly done in skimming exercises). Some less confident students may need special assistance and encouragement in building up skimming skills. These are likely to be the same students who have difficulty as well with the timed reading practice in Part 4.

- After students have completed Part C in each of the exercises, ask them to think about what **lines/phrases/words they read** when they were skimming. Then ask them to check how well they followed the guidelines, or whether they could have done so more effectively.

Additional Activities

- **Re-Reading**
  When students have completed each of the exercises, teachers can ask them to work with the passage as they did in Unit 5:

  1. Is there an overall pattern? If so, what is it?

  2. What is the overall idea?

  3. Mark the main ideas and the important facts and ideas.

  4. Make an outline of the passage on a separate piece of paper.

- **Research project**
  Students can get further skimming practice with a **research assignment**.

  1. Ask students to choose a topic relating to current events. (Check that their topics are current and appropriate.)

  2. Tell them to look for articles (in English) on the Internet relating to their topic. (Remind them that this is when they should skim—to decide which articles to read.)

  3. Each student should prepare a report, written or oral, on the topic. They will need to hand in a list of their sources (the articles they read).

INTRODUCTORY NOTES

Many experts agree that an effective reading program must include fluency practice—that is, work on reading faster. (See Nation 2001, 2009, and Grabe 2009.) This can include extensive reading (Part 1), work on scanning, previewing, and skimming (Part 3), and timed readings—as in this part of the book.

Each of the three units of Part 4 contains eight passages of the same length (600 words). Once students have learned how to time their reading and calculate their reading rate, they can work independently through the units at their own pace. If they fill in the progress charts (on pages 234–236) after each reading, they can compare their initial rate with their rate later in the unit or in the course. It is important for teachers to follow their students' progress closely and respond with praise, encouragement, or advice as appropriate. For this reason, it is best to work on the timed reading passages in class, and not assign them for homework.

For students to develop the confidence needed to increase their reading rate, the texts they work with need to be at an appropriate level, without too many new words. The passages here have been calibrated at a vocabulary level slightly lower than the rest of the book. If students encounter words they are not familiar with, they should stay focused on the overall ideas in the passage and keep reading. They should not stop to look up words in the dictionary.

The comprehension questions that follow each passage are **NOT intended for testing purposes**. They have been included in order to give a rough measure of how well students have understood the passage. This is useful for the students (as well as the teachers), so they can experiment with faster reading speeds and see the effects immediately in terms of comprehension.

Research has shown that rereading can be an effective way for students to build comprehension, vocabulary knowledge, and confidence as readers. If students follow the procedure in the exercises in these units, they will have multiple opportunities to read each passage:

- A. Previewing
- A–B. First reading with timing
- C. Comprehension questions (without looking back at passage)
- D. Second reading
- F. Third reading/skimming (to look for correct answers to questions)

Further activities with a text (after all students have read it) could increase the number of times students read it; though of course, teachers will need to vary the activities and keep alert to signs of weariness with the text or the topic.

It is essential for teachers to have a thorough grasp of the rationale behind reading rate improvement so they can explain it in terms the students will understand. For this reason, teachers should first go through the students' introduction in the Student Book carefully and, if necessary, consult other reference books for clarification.

TEACHING NOTES

Why Read Faster? *(page 228)*

As explained to students, there are three ways they can benefit from improving their reading rate. Teachers should take the time to go over these benefits carefully with the class.

1. *You can be a more efficient reader.*

   Students in most academic settings (and people in many work situations) are faced with a large quantity of reading in English. This can be a problem for many English-language learners who read so slowly that they often have little time left to reflect on and assimilate what they have read. Therefore, it is important for students at all levels to develop reading habits that will allow them to deal with a large amount of reading.

   Furthermore, being able to read faster can make a big difference in extensive reading. Very simply, students who can read faster can get through more books in less time—and the aim of extensive reading is to read as much as possible. In addition, they will probably also enjoy their reading more, so they are likely to read more.

2. *Your knowledge of English can improve.*

   This reason is a logical consequence of the first one. If students read faster and read more, according to research, they can expand their knowledge of vocabulary, syntax, spelling, and writing, and also acquire a sense of how the language is used (see this Teachers Guide to Part 1). Furthermore, aside from these specific language benefits, research has shown that the amount of reading done by a student correlates closely with his or her general academic performance. Students who read a lot tend to be more successful than students who do not read or read little.

3. *Your comprehension can improve.*

   This point may seem to contradict many learners' beliefs that the more slowly and carefully they read, the better they will understand. Studies have shown clearly that this is often not the case. Slow readers make more and longer fixations on each word. This puts more strain on working memory, (also known as short-term memory) since the brain has to try to hold onto many more pieces of information. The result is a slowing down of cognitive processing (the thinking processes necessary to derive meaning from the words on the page). When reading faster, readers make fewer and briefer fixations, with less backtracking, so they can process the text more quickly and efficiently, with less strain on working memory.

   Students may be quite resistant to the idea that they can understand better when they read faster, since it may go against long-held convictions. To help convince them:

   a) Teachers should first explain to students that "reading faster" does not mean speed reading. It means reading somewhat faster than they are now.

   b) Teachers should go through the explanation with students (page 228):

      • Read aloud to students Point 3. *(Your comprehension can improve.)*

      • Tell students to read the sentences with separated words in the example, separating the words. *(What / really / happens /...)*

      • Ask them whether it is easier or harder to understand when the words are separated in this way.

      • Ask them if they had to look back at the beginning of a sentence when they got to the end.

      • Tell them that this problem (difficulty understanding and looking back often) is what happens when we read slowly, word-by-word.

      • Explain to them that when we read this way, our brain has trouble remembering and making sense out of many separate pieces of information.

   Teachers can also point out that the rationale for reading faster relates to the rationale for identifying patterns of organization. As explained on page 172 in Part 3, Unit 4, the brain has trouble holding onto and processing pieces of information that have no apparent order. The order can be of many kinds—numerical, visual, or spatial—or it can be conferred by the structure and meaning of sentences themselves. It is much more difficult, to recognize the structure and meaning in sentences when reading slowly. This is due to the way working memory operates. It can hold only a small number of items (about seven) for a short time. If those items are single words that are processed slowly one-by-one, the reader may not be able to put them together in a meaningful way before they slip from working memory. Because faster readers process more text more quickly, they are better able to put words together into phrases and connect the phrases in a way that enables them to perceive the meaning in the sentences and in the larger text.

Notes *(page 229)*

Teachers should discuss these notes with students and reassure them that not all reading must be fast. Students should aim to have a wide range of reading speeds at their disposal so they can speed up or slow down as necessary, depending on what they are reading and why they are reading it.

There are times when slow reading is appropriate—when reading poetry, complex technical material, or instructions, for example. On the other hand, there are times when it is useful to be able to read quickly—when doing extensive reading, for some homework or class assignments, or in some test situations. More often than not, however, students read everything slowly because that is the only way they are able to read. Learning to read faster will give them more flexibility.

GUIDELINES FOR READING FASTER *(page 229)* ·············

- Teachers should go through this section carefully with students.

  1. *Check your reading habits.*

     These questions should be discussed one-by-one with the whole class. Teachers may already have noticed students who are silently pronouncing words as they read or who follow the words on the page with a finger or a pencil. These students should be alerted to these habits, as they may not be aware of what they are doing.

  2. *Skip or guess unknown words.*

     This is the same advice given to students in Part 1, for the same reasons: Looking up words drastically slows down reading and reinforces the habit of translating. Instead, students should skip over the unknown word or try to quickly guess a general meaning. (At this point, students should already have done Exercises 1–4 in Part 1, Unit 1, pages 4–7, which will help them realize they can skip or guess unknown words.)

  3. *Practice reading faster by timing yourself.*

     Students are introduced here to the idea of timed readings as a way to improve their reading rate. If they have done the reading sprints in Part 1, Unit 3, page 21, they will already have learned how habit can influence the way readers move their eyes across the page and thus the rate at which they read.

Timed Readings

When working on timed readings, students should be encouraged to take risks and keep pushing themselves to read a little faster each time. Teachers should stress the fact that students' scores on the comprehension questions serve only as an indication of the ratio of speed to comprehension in these passages. These scores will not be included in any way in students' grades for the course (though the students' willingness to make a serious effort to increase their rate should be taken into consideration in evaluating students).

If students make more than two errors on the comprehension questions, they may be pushing themselves too much and should perhaps slow down slightly. If they make only one error or none, they could probably read faster with acceptable comprehension and should make an effort to move their eyes ahead more quickly.

Before working with students in Part 4, teachers are strongly advised to follow the procedure themselves for timing and answering the questions. They should then go step-by-step through the Guidelines for Timed Reading on page 230 with students so they will have a good idea what to expect.

Procedure for Practice Exercise *(page 231)*

- When the whole class is ready, students should write the **exact starting time** at the top of the passage. If there is a large clock in the classroom or students have watches, they can note the time themselves. If not, teachers can write the starting time on the board.

- Students should follow the instructions exactly, including **previewing**, and they should **read to the end** of the passage as quickly as possible with understanding.

- When they finish, students should **write the exact time**. If there is no clock and they do not have watches, they can raise their hands when they finish and the teacher can write the time for each student on the board.

- Students should time themselves only while reading the passage, and not while answering the questions.

- After they finish reading the passage, students should **turn the page** and circle the best answers to the questions. Their answers should be chosen according to what they remember from the text. They should **not look back** at the passage.

- When they have answered all the questions as best they can, students should **read the passage again**, pushing themselves to read faster. Then they can look at their answers to the questions and revise them if necessary.

- At this point, students calculate their **reading time** (finishing time minus starting time), find their **reading rate** on the table on page 233, and write it in the progress chart on page 234. They also check their answers to the questions and write their **comprehension score** (number of correct answers) in the progress chart.

GENERAL GUIDELINES

- Students should **not stop to look up words** or write them down. Vocabulary development is important, but here students should be focused on rate improvement. Teachers can ask students later to look back at the passage and learn new words (see Part 2, Unit 2).

- Every week, teachers should **check students' progress**, both their reading rate and their comprehension scores and give encouragement or advice accordingly.

- Students should be reminded regularly to **preview** before they read. They may need to be assured that it is worth investing a few seconds in previewing, as it will help them read faster afterwards.

- When students move from one unit to the next, they may find that their reading rate drops at first because of the change in content matter. They may need to be reassured that this is natural, and that their rate will probably pick up again after a few passages.

- During rate improvement sessions, the **passages should not be used for other purposes**. If students think they need to worry about vocabulary or other aspects of the text, they will not feel free to push themselves to read faster. After the students have all read a passage, however, it can be used for discussion, comprehension skills practice, or vocabulary learning.

Additional Activities

Teachers who wish to give their students further practice in timed readings can provide the classroom with a set of books with timed reading passages (such as *Reading for Speed and Fluency 2,* by Paul Nation and Casey Malarcher).

UNIT 1
Harry Houdini: The Life of an Escape Artist

This unit tells the story of Harry Houdini, born as Erich Weiss in Hungary in 1874, who became a world-famous magician and escape artist. Though the narrative takes place in the past, many students may be able to relate to his difficult situation as an immigrant and an outsider in the United States—not only Hungarian, but also Jewish—and sympathize with his desire to make his mark on the world.

When all the students have finished the unit, teachers could follow up with further readings and discussion about Houdini, about immigrants (or, Jewish immigrants) in the United States, about past forms of entertainment—magicians, escape artists, or circuses—or other themes relating to the readings.

UNIT 2
Making a Living

In this unit, students will read about eight very different and sometimes unusual ways of making a living. Some of them are specific to a place, while others are common in many countries. Any of the readings could be followed by discussion and/or further readings relating to the job and/or the place.

When reading the first few passages of this unit, students may find their reading rate slows down, since these readings are descriptive and somewhat more complex in structure and concept than the passages in the first unit, which were more straightforward narratives. However, once students get used to the structure and type of content, their speed should pick up again. If not, teachers should encourage students to push themselves to read faster.

Additional Activities

- **Reaction report**
  After a timed reading session, students could be asked to write a brief report about a passage they have just read. They should be encouraged to express themselves freely about any aspect of the passage that struck them, not just about the job at the focus of the reading, but also about the lives of the people who do the job.

- **Research project**
  When all the students have finished the unit, teachers can ask them to choose a job to research. It could be a job that is typical of their native city or country, or a job that they think would be interesting. Teachers should encourage students to be creative and to choose unusual jobs.

UNIT 3
Better Lives in a Better World

This unit is the most dense with information and ideas, but at this point, students should be ready to deal with the more academic style and content of these passages. As with Unit 2, teachers can use the topics as the focus of further discussion or research.

When students have all read the passages, they can be used for further work with vocabulary or comprehension skills.

Planning a Course with *More Reading Power 3*

Using the Book in Different Contexts

The materials in this book were designed to take approximately 35–40 hours of class time, though this may vary considerably according to the level of the students and the amount of homework assigned. Whatever the teaching situation, teachers should **use all four parts of the book regularly**. It is also important never to spend more than 20–30 minutes on one type of activity and to spend less than that on exercises that could become tedious.

Suggested course plans for various situations:

- **Intensive integrated skills class (2–3 hours, five days a week)**
  Use *More Reading Power 3* for about 45 minutes, three to four times a week, dividing the time evenly among the four parts. Homework assignments can focus on extensive reading and additional activities, such as preparing for presentations and research projects relating to readings in the book.

- **Integrated skills class (3 hours per week)**
  Use *More Reading Power 3* for one-third of the class time—about one hour altogether, divided evenly among the four parts. Homework assignments can include exercises in Parts 2 and 3, after the exercise type has been introduced in class.

- **Reading class (2 hours per week)**
  Use all four parts of *More Reading Power 3* in each class, dividing the time evenly. Homework assignments can focus on extensive reading and additional activities such as preparing for presentations and research projects relating to readings in the book.

- **Reading lab**
  Instruct students in how to use each of the parts of *More Reading Power 3* before they begin working independently in that part. Tell them to divide their time evenly among the four parts, including extensive reading.

Homework Assignments

The amount of homework teachers assign will depend on the amount of class time they can devote to work on reading, and on the level of autonomy of the students. In any case, students should never be assigned as homework types of exercises that they are not already familiar with.

Though teachers can assign **extensive reading** for homework, they should be sure to spend time on it in the classroom as well. If students only do extensive reading outside the classroom, they may get the impression that it is less important. (See the Introduction to Part 1.)

In general, teachers should not assign **timed reading passages** from Part 4 for homework. Students are more likely to follow the procedures correctly and concentrate on reading faster in the classroom.

Understanding the Rationale

Before starting each part of the book, teachers should read the relevant part of this Teacher's Guide. Understanding the approach taken in the book is essential for using it successfully in the classroom.

Likewise, it is vital for students also to understand why they are doing each type of exercise and how it will help them improve their reading. No matter how pressed for time teachers may feel, it is worth taking a few minutes to go through the explanations in the book, reinforcing them as necessary with additional information, research, anecdotes. Students should be allowed to ask questions or express doubts, particularly about aspects of reading that may be new to them, such as extensive reading and reading rate improvement.

Teachers who are using the book for the first time will have a better understanding of the procedures involved if they actually do each type of exercise before introducing it to the class. This will make it easier to explain the rationale and the procedure to the students.

Sample Syllabus

The syllabus included here is intended only to give a rough indication of how work in the four parts of the book can be distributed over a 13-week semester. Teachers will need to adjust the pace and distribution according to the needs of their students and the requirements of their teaching situation.

Tests are available in the *More Reading Power 3 Test Booklet* for each type of exercise. These can be given any time after students have completed work on the related exercises in the student book. The tests can also be used for extra practice on a given skill. In the syllabus, a testing schedule is indicated for Part 4, but not for the other parts, because progress is likely to vary considerably.

Notes

- *Review vocabulary* is a reminder to teachers to take time for vocabulary review, not only of the vocabulary for that lesson or that week, but also from earlier weeks. This should include vocabulary from all parts of the book, from their reading or from class activities. Teachers should check that students continue to make effective use of their vocabulary notebooks and study cards.

- *Prepare presentation* may refer only to those students who are due to give a presentation that week. If there is time in the course for two presentations per student, they would be preparing presentations in weeks 5, 6, and 7 as well.

- *Writing activity* refers to Book Reports, Book Files, or other writing activities relating to extensive reading. They are indicated here for the middle and end of the semester, but teachers may prefer to ask students to do them in class or at another point in the course.

- When working on the timed readings in Part 4, teachers should allow students to work at their own pace. This may mean that some students will finish the units sooner than others. If they complete all the readings early, teachers can give them additional material for rate practice or have them read in their extensive-reading books. Students who fall behind the schedule on the syllabus should be encouraged to try to catch up.

	PART 1 Extensive Reading	PART 2 Vocabulary Building	PART 3 Comprehension Skills	PART 4 Reading Fluency
SAMPLE SYLLABUS				
Week 1	Intro to book, Questionnaire Unit 1 Intro, Exs. 1–4	Unit 1 Intro, Exs. 1–4	Unit 1 Intro, Scanning, Exs. 1, 2 Unit 1 FOV, Exs. 1–3	Intro to Part 4, Unit 1, Ex. 1
Homework			Unit 1 FOV, Exs. 3–6	
Week 2	Unit 2, Ex. 1 Unit 3, Choosing a Book, Ex. 1	Check homework Unit 1, Pr.1, Exs. 5, 6 Unit 2 Intro, Exs. 1, 2	Check homework Unit 1, Scanning, Exs. 3, 4, 5 Unit 2 Intro, Pr. Ex., Exs. 1, 2	Unit 1 Exercises
Homework	Get book Read in book	Unit 2, Exs. 3, 4 Review vocab.	Unit 1 FOV, Exs. 4–6	
Week 3	Unit 2, Ex. 2 Unit 3, Finding Your Reading Rate Reading Circles	Check homework Unit 2 Intro, Exs. 3, 4 Study Cards, Ex. 6	Check homework Unit 1 Previewing, Exs. 6, 7 Unit 2, Exs. 3, 5, 6 Unit 2 FOV, Exs. 1, 2	Unit 1 Exercises
Homework	Read in book	Review vocab	Unit 2 FOV, Exs. 3, 4	
Week 4	Unit 3, Reading Sprints Reading Circles Other activities	Check homework Unit 3 Intro, Pr. 1, Exs. 1, 2	Check homework Unit 1, Exs. 8, 9 Unit 2, Exs. 7, 8 Unit 3 Intro Topics, Pr. 1, Exs. 1, 2	Unit 1 Test
Homework	Read in book	Unit 3, Exs. 3, 4 Review vocab	Unit 2 FOV, Exs. 5, 6	
Week 5	Reading Circles Other activities	Check homework Unit 3, Exs. 5, 6 Unit 4 Intro, Exs. 1, 2	Check homework Unit 3, Exs. 3–5	Unit 2 Exercises
Homework	Read in book	Unit 4, Exs. 3, 4, 5 Review vocab	Unit 3 FOV, Exs. 1–3	
Week 6	Book Conferences Reading Circles Other activities	Check homework Unit 3, Pr. 2, Exs. 7, 8 Unit 4, Ex. 6	Check homework Unit 3, Exs. 6, 7 Following Ideas, Ex. 8 Unit 4 Intro, Exs. 1–3	Unit 2 Exercises
Homework	Read in book Writing Activity	Unit 4, Exs. 7, 8 Review vocab	Unit 3 Exs. 9–11 Unit 3 FOV, Exs. 4–6	
Week 7	Book Conferences Reading Circles Other activities	Check homework Unit 4, Ex. 9 Unit 5 Intro, Pr., Ex. 1	Check homework Unit 4, Exs. 4–7	Unit 2 Exercises
Homework	Read in book Writing Activity	Unit 4, Ex. 10 Review vocab	Unit 4, Ex. 8 Unit 4 FOV, Exs. 1–3	

	PART 1 Extensive Reading	PART 2 Vocabulary Building	PART 3 Comprehension Skills	PART 4 Reading Fluency
SAMPLE SYLLABUS				
Week 8	Book Conferences Reading Circles Other activities	Check homework Unit 5, Exs. 2, 3	Check homework Unit 5 Intro, Pr. 1, 2, Exs. 1, 2	Unit 2 Test
Homework	Read in book Prepare presentation	Unit 5, Ex. 4 Review vocab	Unit 4 FOV, Exs. 4–6	

Week 9	Book Presentations
	Reading Circles
	Other activities
		Check homework
		Unit 5,
		  Coll. in Ac.
		  writing, Exs. 5, 6
			Check homework
			Unit 5, Ex. 3
			Unit 6 Intro, Exs.
			1, 2
				Unit 3 Exercises

Homework	Read in book Prepare presentation	Review vocab	Unit 5, Ex. 4 Unit 5 FOV, Exs. 1–3	

Week 10	Book Presentations
	Other activities
		Check homework
		Unit 5, Ex. 7
		Unit 6,
		  Key Parts, Pr., Ex. 1
		  Signal Words, Ex. 2
			Check homework
			Unit 5, Ex. 5
			Unit 6 Intro, Exs.
			1, 2
				Unit 3 Exercises

Homework	Read in book Prepare presentation	Unit 6, Ex. 3 Review vocab	Unit 5, Ex. 6 Unit 5 FOV, Exs. 4–6	
Week 11	Book Presentations Reading Circles Other activities	Check homework Unit 6, Pronouns, Exs. 4, 5, 6	Check homework Unit 6, Exs. 3, 4	Unit 3 Exercises
Homework	Read in book Prepare presentation Writing Activity	Review vocab	Unit 6 FOV, Exs. 1–3	
Week 12	Book Presentations Reading Circles Other activities	Check homework Unit 6, Synonyms Exs. 7, 8	Check homework Unit 6, Exs. 5, 6	Unit 3 Exercises
Homework	Read in book Writing Activity	Review vocab	Unit 6 FOV, Exs. 4–6 Research reports or other activities	
Week 13	Reading survey or other activity	Vocab presentations or other activities	Research reports or other activities	Unit 3 Test

MORE READING
POWER 3
ANSWER KEY

PART 1 — EXTENSIVE READING

(Answers may vary.)

Exercise 1 *(page 4)*

a. a young woman, her husband, her children—a boy and a girl
b. She doesn't care about them or love them. She doesn't like being with them, so she feels impatient with them.
c. The children understand that she doesn't love them, and they don't love her.
d. They pretend to care for each other, but they all know it is not real.
e. Other people think that she is a good mother and they are a loving family.

Exercise 2 *(page 5)*

a. There's a feeling of anxiety or worry about money.
b. Yes, in a bank. Probably he would be considered successful, since he is paid well.
c. Yes, part-time in a real-estate office. She's not very successful because she doesn't make many sales.
d. She looks for a way to make money online.
e. The lifestyle of wealthy people and the money to support it.
f. Answers may vary.

Exercise 3 *(page 6)*

(Any word or phrase that is grammatically and collocationally correct is acceptable.)

1. advantages
2. beautiful
3. ended
4. ready
5. wasting
6. seemed
7. able
8. true
9. large
10. grass

Exercise 4 *(page 7)*

1. games
2. invited
3. time
4. earned
5. worry
6. activities
7. make
8. lined
9. word
10. put

UNIT 2
Fiction and Nonfiction

(Answers will vary.)

UNIT 3
Books

(Answers will vary.)

PART 2 — VOCABULARY BUILDING

UNIT 1
Making Good Use of the Dictionary

Exercise 2 *(page 34)*

B.
1. enjoy, level
2. hear, reach
3. limit, thin
4. fruit, cruel
5. much, choose
6. fact, match
7. organize, gift
8. doubt, amount

Exercise 5 *(page 39)*

A.
1. adverb
2. adjective
3. noun
4. adjective
5. verb
6. noun

Exercise 6 *(page 42)*

A.
1. verb
   1 to affect someone or involve him/her.
2. noun
   2 something important that worries you or involves you
3. adjective
   3 involved in something
4. adjective
   1 worried about something important
5. noun
   1 a feeling of worry about something important

B. They all include the idea of worry about or involvement in something.

Exercise 7 *(page 43)*

1. a. growth, development
   b. system
2. a. growing
   b. way
   c. depressed
   d. global

3. a. of
   b. as . . . as

Exercise 8 *(page 44)*

1. a. for
   b. about
   c. for
   d. for
   e. with
   f. about
2. a. primary/main/major
   b. main/primary/major
   c. major/primary/main
3. himself

UNIT 2
Learning New Vocabulary from Your Reading

(Answers will vary.)

UNIT 3
Guessing Meaning from Context

Exercise 1 *(page 59)*

1. noun
   the top, the time of most success
2. phrasal verb
   to get larger
3. adjective
   very dirty or rude
4. verb
   get smaller
5. phrasal verb
   to be found
6. verb
   to be worth something special or something more

Exercise 2 *(page 60)*

1. prepositional phrase
   at some later time
2. noun
   water that forms on things outdoors at night
3. adjective
   wet
4. adverb
   only a little
5. verb
   tied
6. verb
   to sew or cover a hole in clothes

Exercise 3 *(page 61)*

1. verb
   to stop or slow down
2. noun
   a structure covered with glass or plastic where plants can grow in cold weather
3. verbal phrase
   to cause
4. adjective
   not busy or occupied in any way
5. verbal phrase
   to consider, think about something
6. adjective
   cold

Exercise 4 *(page 62)*

1. prepositional phrase
   later, in the future
2. adjective
   excellent
3. noun
   amount of something that is produced
4. verbal phrase
   to manage not to be discovered or punished
5. adverb
   in a way that is embarrassed or clumsy
6. verb
   to take something quickly and violently

Exercise 5 *(page 63)*

1. a. adjective
      not bothered by anyone
   b. verb
      to open, usually a book
2. a. noun
      a group (informal)
   b. phrasal verb
      to spend time together (informal)

Exercise 6 *(page 64)*

1. a. verb
      to hate
   b. noun
      a hotel or place where people rent rooms
2. a. verb
      to ask for something you want very much
   b. noun
      building and land used by a store or business

Exercise 7 (page 66)

1. noun
   a special kind of taxi van or large car
2. noun
   a kind of reusable ticket or pass for travel on buses and/or trains
3. noun
   a ticket or fine (money you have to pay)

Exercise 8 (page 67)

1. noun
   dump (public place for a town or city's garbage/trash)
2. noun
   fish farms
3. verb
   to recycle

UNIT 4
Word Parts

Exercise 1 (page 69)

(Additional word will vary. These are some possibilities. Any word that includes the root is acceptable.)

1. Root: locus   New Word: location
2. Root: meter   New Word: metric
3. Root: dict   New Word: dictate
4. Root: invent   New Word: invent
5. Root: cycle   New Word: cycle
6. Root: path   New Word: empathy
7. Root: form   New Word: formation
8. Root: nunc   New Word: announcement
9. Root: lit   New Word: literature
10. Root: duct   New Word: induction
11. Root: ject   New Word: inject
12. Root: form   New Word: formal
13. Root: invent   New Word: inventive
14. Root: duct   New Word: production
15. Root: nunc   New Word: pronounce
16. Root: dict   New Word: dictionary
17. Root: geo   New Word: geology
18. Root: port   New Word: import
19. Root: nation   New Word: nationality
20. Root: cycle   New Word: cyclical

Exercise 2 (page 70)

A.
1. in-
2. mis-
3. dis-
4. un-
5. im-
6. dis-
7. un-
8. non-
9. in-
10. mis-
11. im-
12. non-

C. They all make the word negative.

Exercise 3 (page 71)

A.
1. bi-
2. tri-
3. cent-
4. uni-
5. cent-
6. tri-
7. uni-
8. tri-
9. bi-
10. uni-

(Order may vary.)

C.
1. Prefix: uni-   Meaning: one
2. Prefix: bi-   Meaning: two
3. Prefix: tri-   Meaning: three
4. Prefix: cent-   Meaning: hundred

Exercise 4 (page 72)

A.
1. pre-
2. out-
3. under-
4. re-
5. over-
6. under-
7. over-
8. pre-
9. out-
10. pre-
11. re-
12. out-
13. re-
14. under-
15. re-
16. over-

C. (Order may vary.)
1. Prefix: pre-
   Meaning: before, earlier
2. Prefix: out-
   Meaning: more, better
3. Prefix: under-
   Meaning: less than, lower, not enough
4. Prefix: re-
   Meaning: again, back, as before
5. Prefix: over-
   Meaning: too much

Exercise 5 (page 73)

A.
1. Word to cross out: regular
   Prefix: re-
   Meaning: again, back, as before
2. Word to cross out: until
   Prefix: un-
   Meaning: not
3. Word to cross out: pressure
   Prefix: pre-
   Meaning: before, earlier
4. Word to cross out: comeback
   Prefix: com-
   Meaning: with, together
5. Word to cross out: miserable
   Prefix: mis-
   Meaning: not, bad, wrong
6. Word to cross out: distance
   Prefix: dis-
   Meaning: not, lack of

7. Word to cross out: industry
   Prefix: in-
   Meaning: not

8. Word to cross out: bitter
   Prefix: bi-
   Meaning: two

(go to next column)

Exercise 6 *(page 74)*

A.

	Word	Part of Speech	Root (- prefix)	Part of Speech of Root
1.	unfaithful	adjective	faith	noun
2.	strangely	adverb	strange	adjective
3.	powerless	adjective	power	noun or verb
4.	restful	adjective	rest	noun or verb
5.	broadly	adverb	broad	adjective
6.	unbelievable	adjective	believe	verb
7.	widely	adverb	wide	adjective
8.	watchful	adjective	watch	verb
9.	childless	adjective	child	noun
10.	invaluable	adjective	value	noun or verb
11.	careful	adjective	care	noun or verb
12.	noticeable	adjective	notice	noun or verb

B.

	Suffixes	Part of Speech Words with Suffix	Part of Speech Words without Suffix
	(Order may vary.)		
1.	-ly	adverb	adjective
2.	-ful	adjective	noun or verb
3.	-less	adjective	noun
4.	-able	adjective	noun or verb

Exercise 7 *(page 75)*

A.

	Word	Part of Speech	Root (- prefix)	Part of Speech of Root
1.	annoying	adjective	annoy	verb
2.	influential	adjective	influence	noun or verb
3.	demanding	adjective	demand	verb
4.	expressive	adjective	express	verb
5.	independent	adjective	depend	verb
6.	existing	adjective	exist	verb
7.	insensitive	adjective	sense	noun or verb
8.	judgmental	adjective	judge	noun or verb
9.	confident	adjective	confide	verb
10.	informal	adjective	form	noun or verb
11.	massive	adjective	mass	noun
12.	environmental	adjective	environment	noun

B.

	Suffixes	Part of Speech Words with Suffix	Part of Speech Words without Suffix
	(Order may vary.)		
1.	-ing	adjective	verb
2.	-al	adjective	verb
3.	-ive	adjective	noun or verb
4.	-ent	adjective	verb

Exercise 8 (page 76)

A.

Word	Part of Speech	Root (- prefix)	Part of Speech of Root
1. generalize	verb	general	adjective
2. addition	noun	add	verb
3. impossibility	noun	possible	adjective
4. invention	noun	invent	verb
5. weaken	verb	weak	adjective
6. specialize	verb	special	adjective
7. freshness	noun	fresh	adjective
8. reproduction	noun	reproduce	verb
9. simplicity	noun	simple	adjective
10. modernize	verb	modern	adjective
11. preparation	noun	prepare	verb
12. lengthen	verb	length	noun
13. popularity	noun	popular	adjective
14. forgetfulness	noun	forget	verb

B. (Order may vary.)

Suffixes	Part of Speech Words with Suffix	Part of Speech Words without Suffix
1. -ize	verb	adjective
2. -ion	noun	verb
3. -ity	noun	adjective
4. -en	verb	adjective or noun
5. -ness	noun	adjective

Exercise 9 (page 78)

	Noun	Verb	Adjective	Negative Adjective	Adverb
1.	reason	reason	reasonable	unreasonable	reasonably
2.	freshness	freshen	fresh	X	freshly
3.	possibility	X	possible	impossible	possibly
4.	relation, relationship, relative, relativity	relate	related, relative	unrelated	relatively
5.	preparation	prepare	prepared	unprepared	X
6.	service	serve	serviceable	X	X
7.	sense	sense, sensibility, sensitivity	sensible, sensitive	nonsensical, insensitive	sensibly, sensitively
8.	profit	profit	profitable	unprofitable, nonprofit	profitably
9.	realization, reality, realism	realize	real, realistic	unreal, unrealistic	really
10.	limit	limit	limited	unlimited	X
11.	operation	operate	operational	X	operationally
12.	specialization, specialist, speciality	specialize	special, specialized	X	specially

Exercise 10 *(page 79)*

	Noun	Verb	Adjective	Negative Adjective	Adverb
1.	organization	organize	organized, organizational	unorganized, disorganized	X
2.	recognition	recognize	recognizable	unrecognizable	recognizably
3.	product, production, produce	produce	productive	unproductive	productively
4.	unity	unite	united	X	X
5.	substance	substantiate	substantial	insubstantial	substantially
6.	suggestion	suggest	suggestive	X	X
7.	settlement	settle	settled	unsettled	X
8.	equality	equal, equalize	equal	unequal	equally
9.	value	value	valuable	invaluable*	X
10.	development	develop	developing, developed, developmental	undeveloped	developmentally
11.	account	count, account (for)	accountable	unaccountable	unaccountably
12.	consideration	consider	considerable, considerate	inconsiderate	considerably, inconsiderately

*The literal meaning of *invaluable* is negative—"without a value or price"—but it is used to express a positive meaning—"very useful."

Exercise 11 *(page 80)*

	Noun	Verb	Adjective	Negative Adjective	Adverb
1.	demand	demand	demanding	undemanding	X
2.	dependence, independence, dependent	depend	dependent	independent	independently
3.	form, formality	form, formalize	formal	informal	formally
4.	manager	manage	manageable	unmanageable	manageably
5.	ability, disability	disable	able	disabled	ably
6.	agreement	agree	agreeable	disagreeable	agreeably
7.	simplicity, simplification	simplify	simple	X	simply
8.	notice	notice	noticeable	unnoticeable	noticeably
9.	expression	express	expressive	inexpressive	expressively
10.	report, reporter	report	reported	unreported	reportedly
11.	popularity	popularize	popular	unpopular	popularly
12.	length	lengthen	lengthy	X	X

Exercise 12 (page 81)

	Noun	Verb	Adjective	Negative Adjective	Adverb
1.	generalization, generality	generalize	general	X	generally
2.	belief	believe	believable	unbelievable	unbelievably
3.	office	officiate	official	unofficial	officially
4.	perfection	perfect	perfect	imperfect	perfectly
5.	power	power, empower	powerful	powerless	powerfully
6.	existence	exist	existing	nonexistent	X
7.	weakness	weaken	weak	X	weakly
8.	influence	influence	influential	X	influentially
9.	addition	add	additional	X	additionally
10.	surety	ensure	sure	unsure	surely
11.	rest	rest	restful	restless	restfully, restlessly
12.	prediction	predict	predictable	unpredictable	predictably

UNIT 5
Collocations

Exercise 1 (page 86)

A.
1. slow down
2. signed up
3. bring up
4. figure out
5. take up
6. carried on
7. is going on
8. bring about

B.
1. take up
2. bring up
3. was going on
4. bring about
5. slowed down
6. sign up
7. figure out
8. carried on

Exercise 2 (page 87)

A.
1. severe weather
2. full story
3. dramatic sight
4. terrible shock
5. cheap source
6. new opportunities
7. close contact
8. technological improvement

B.
1. terrible shock
2. technological improvement
3. dramatic sight
4. severe weather
5. cheap source
6. full story
7. close contact
8. new opportunities

Exercise 3 (page 88)

A.
1. right to
2. doubts about
3. problem with
4. advantage over
5. position as
6. lack of
7. limit to
8. interest in

B.
1. interest in
2. limit to
3. lack of
4. advantage over
5. problem with
6. position as
7. doubts about
8. right to

Exercise 4 (page 89)

A.
1. take charge of
2. making little progress in
3. have access to
4. raise money for
5. took care of
6. make a difference in
7. ran the business
8. join some kind of club

B.
1. make a difference in
2. take care of
3. joined a club
4. making progress
5. ran a/his business
6. raise money for
7. took charge of
8. have access to

D.
1. have access to Internet/basic health care
2. make a difference in the company/the results
3. make progress in the war on crime/make progress on his thesis
4. raise money for the school trip/the new sports center
5. take care of all the reservations/my house plants
6. take charge of their learning/the situation

Exercise 5 (page 91)

1. argues that, effect on
2. raises important issues, current theories
3. suggest that, carried out
4. deal with, set up

5. based on, a variety of
6. reach our goal, a great deal of
7. so far, support our theory, effect on
8. a number of, such as

Exercise 6 (page 91)

1. according to, serves an important purpose
2. in recent years, dramatically changed
3. according to, current theory
4. focusing on
5. results suggest, little difference
6. solve the problem, in the long run, focus on, possible causes
7. data show, a number of, possible causes
8. a number of, main reason

Exercise 7 (page 92)

A.
1. suggests that, carry out, a number of, main reason, focused on, effect on, a variety of, solve problems
2. argue that, in recent years, carried out, a great deal, based on, serve a number of purposes

B.
1. the best way, kinds of, working together, better than, a group of, a wider range of, in addition, studies show, tend to, take risks, as a whole, as a result
2. an important role, find out, made it possible, special equipment, the results of these studies

---

Unit 6
Structure and Reference

Exercise 1 (page 94)

Bus Passes in Oslo

1. <u>Various kinds of bus passes</u> <u>are</u> available in Oslo. <u>Some</u> <u>are</u> good for a day, while

      S   V   S V

<u>others</u> <u>are</u> for three days or a week. <u>They</u> all <u>allow</u> unlimited travel on the local

  S   V   S   V

buses and subway. <u>These passes</u> <u>are</u> useful for tourists <u>who</u> <u>want</u> to visit different parts of

               S   V   S   V

the city. <u>There</u> <u>is</u> also another kind of weekly pass <u>that</u> <u>allows</u> unlimited travel on buses

          S V   S   V

and trains and boats anywhere in the country. <u>This pass</u> <u>is</u> quite expensive, but <u>it</u> <u>is</u> worth
                                         S   V   S V

getting if <u>you</u> <u>are planning</u> to move around the country a lot. Otherwise, <u>it</u> <u>is</u> better to pay
              S   V

separately for each trip.

Foreign Drivers in the United States

2. <u>Foreign drivers in the United States</u> <u>should pay attention</u> to the rules of the road. If
               S   V

<u>they</u> <u>do not follow</u> the rules carefully, <u>they</u> <u>may get</u> into trouble. For instance, <u>the police</u>
  S   V   S   V   S

<u>are</u> usually very strict about the speed limit. <u>Drivers going only five miles per hour over</u>
V   S

the limit <u>may just get</u> a warning. However, <u>drivers going ten miles per hour or more over</u>
             V   S

the limit <u>will get</u> a ticket. <u>The cost of tickets</u> <u>can vary</u>, though <u>it</u> <u>may be</u> as much as $250.
          V   S   V   S V

Furthermore, <u>information about all tickets</u> <u>is put into</u> the police computer system. <u>This</u>
                     S   V   S

<u>can cause</u> problems for drivers if, for example, <u>they</u> <u>want</u> to rent a car.
V   S   V

<u>The car rental companies</u> <u>can find out</u> about the tickets and <u>refuse</u> to rent to those drivers.
        S   V   V

Exercise 2 *(page 96)*

Unexpected Effects

Which finger do you use to press a doorbell? The answer may depend on your age.
People who are over thirty will almost certainly do it with their index finger. <u>However</u>,
those who are under thirty will probably use their thumbs. Young people have spent
many hours exercising their thumbs when sending text messages or playing video games.
Thanks to all that exercise, their thumbs have become stronger and more skillful. That is
why they often use their thumbs instead of their index fingers.

Skillful thumbs are only one of the many unexpected effects of new technology. <u>In fact</u>, today's new products are influencing not only physical skills, but also mental skills.
<u>Most of the time</u> people are not aware of what's happening. They change their behavior
as necessary, little by little. The new skills they develop may include texting, <u>for example</u>,
or how to make an online flight reservation.

As for the old skills, <u>most of the time</u> people do not even realize what they have lost.
<u>For instance</u>, how many people can do mental arithmetic these days? It is rarely necessary
with calculators in every office and on every phone or computer. And with GPS in many
cars, there is little need to be able to follow directions or read a map.

Some researchers are concerned about the consequences of losing the old mental
skills. If GPS stopped functioning, <u>for example</u>, would anyone know how to find their
way around? <u>More importantly</u>, since the collapse of all technology is unlikely, scientists
wonder about our brains. What will happen to them if we no longer exercise them in the
same way?

Exercise 3 *(page 96)*

The Early Cinema

The cinema had its beginnings at the end of the 19th century in the United States.
It grew out of several earlier forms of entertainment, <u>including</u> theater, and out of the
technology developed for so-called "peep shows."

Peep Shows

In the 1890's peep shows were popular in many American cities. In a peep show, a film was viewed through a small opening in a machine that was created for that purpose.

Among those who worked on peep shows was Thomas Edison, who invented a peep show machine in 1894. He then opened several special shops for his machines, where customers paid 25 cents to move from one machine to another and view short films.

New Technology

In these same years, however, other inventors began to look ahead. They realized that there was a basic limit to the peep show machines: Only one person at a time could look at a film. They wanted to improve the technology so they could show films to more people, so they worked on developing film projectors.

Edison did not become involved in this development because he believed he could make money with his peep show machines. In fact, he missed a major opportunity.

Entertainment for Everyone

By 1895, the first film projectors were in use in theaters, halls, and fairs. From the point of view of the producer, film production had several important advantages over theater or music hall productions. First of all, the material was recorded. Once the film was produced, there was no need for the actors, singers, lighting people, or make-up people. Furthermore, each film could be shown to much larger numbers of people. In other words, a successful film could make a lot more profit.

Audiences were also immediately enthusiastic about these early films. Unlike the peep shows, the cinema experience could be shared with others. And unlike the theater, where audiences were limited, there were almost no limits to the number of viewers for a film. This was the real beginning of the mass entertainment of the 20th century.

Exercise 4 *(page 98)*

Pedicabs

A pedicab is a small cab that is pulled by a bicycle. It has been popular in Asian
<small>s</small>

countries for many years. About ten years ago, it was introduced in Denver, Colorado.
<small>s</small>

Before long, there were pedicabs in many American cities in the United States. These cabs do not

take the place of taxis because people use them mainly just for short rides. The passengers
<small>o</small>

of pedicabs are often people who do not want to walk because they are well-dressed for
<small>s</small>

an evening event. Tourists also take them as a fun and unusual way to get around a city.
<small>o</small>

The drivers of pedicabs are usually friendly students with strong legs. They pay the
<small>s</small>

owner of the cabs a certain amount to use one for a day or evening. Any money they earn
<small>s</small>

from passengers above that amount is their own. Typically, a pedicab driver earns about
<small>P</small>

as much as he or she would earn by working in a restaurant. However, students who have
<small>s</small> <small>s</small>

chosen pedicabs say they prefer this kind of work. It may be more tiring, but they enjoy
<small>s</small> <small>s</small> <small>s</small>

being outdoors. They also like the fact that no one is telling them what to do.
<small>s</small> <small>o</small>

Exercise 5 *(page 99)*

Is Txting Bad 4 English?

People tend to feel strongly about texting. Some people love it, while others hate it. Among the haters, some have expressed their opinion in very strong terms. One British journalist said that "texters are doing to our language what Genghis Khan did to his neighbors 800 years ago. They are destroying . . . our punctuation . . . our sentences . . . our vocabulary. And they must be stopped."*

This is not the first time that people have said that technology was bad for language. In the 15th century, some scholars opposed the invention of the printing press. Common people should not read books, these scholars argued, or the language might begin to reflect their common ways of thinking and speaking. More recently, the telegraph and then the telephone were also viewed as tools of linguistic destruction. And yet, the English language has survived.

In fact, there is reason to think that texting will be no more harmful to the language than any of those past inventions. Research has shown that many of the claims made by text haters are not based on reality. They especially dislike the way words in messages may be shortened, and numbers and symbols used instead of words. However, only about 20 percent or fewer messages actually do contain these shorter forms. In most messages, traditional spellings and whole sentences are used. The reason for this is practical: the majority of senders are not teenagers, but schools, banks, and companies. They want to make sure they will be understood.

Among texters who do use the shortened forms, certain forms appear frequently, such as c = see, u = you, and 4 = for. However, there is also a lot of variation. That is because texting can actually be quite creative and fun. It could be considered a kind of word play, like doing crosswords or puzzles.

Exercise 6 *(page 101)*

The Tuaregs: From Nomads to Farmers

For the Tuareg people of north-central Africa, life has changed dramatically in recent years. Historically, the Tuaregs led the life of nomads, people with no permanent home. They traveled across the Sahara Desert in caravans of camels, carrying goods between Arab Africa in the north and black Africa in the south.

Neither Arab nor black African, the Tuaregs were a light-skinned Berber people who had a culture and a language of their own. To Europeans, they were the "blue men" of the desert because they dressed all in blue. They were known for their great skill in finding their way across the open desert, with only the stars to guide them.

They were also known for their independent spirit. In fact, they loved the nomad way of life which allowed them to come and go as they chose. National borders had no meaning for them in the desert. During the 19th century, Africa was divided up and ruled by various European countries, but this did not affect the Tuaregs, who continued to move freely. In the 20th century, however, many of the new African nations closed their borders which forced the Tuaregs to limit their travels and trade.

At the same time, another big change had come to the area. People began to use motor vehicles for travel across the desert, which meant the Tuareg camel caravans lost their important role. Then came the great drought (dry weather) of the 1970s and 1980s. Many animals died, including the Tuaregs' camels. Their old way of life was now definitively over.

In recent years, some of the Tuaregs have managed to make a new life for themselves as farmers. They have settled near the old water holes, such as Timia, in central Niger.

---

*John Humphreys, "I h8 txt msgs: How texting is wrecking our language," *The Daily Mail,* 24 September 2007.

In the past, it was just a (place in the middle of the desert) where travelers stopped to rest. Now it has a population of about 10,000. Most of (the people) who live there were nomads in the past, but now they make a living from their fruit and vegetable gardens. They grow (oranges, grapefruits, pomegranates, dates, and corn,) which they send by truck to Agadez, the nearest city.

Exercise 7 *(page 102)*

1. Scientists have found evidence of <u>communities</u> living in Kunda, northern Estonia around 6500 BCE. These <u>groups of people</u> had not yet started farming, but lived by hunting and fishing.
2. In the last two hundred years, <u>Estonia</u> has been occupied and ruled by forces from Germany, Sweden, Russia, and other countries. <u>This small eastern European nation</u> has had a difficult and often violent past.
3. During the 20th century, one <u>war</u> after another brought suffering to Estonians. They were involved in <u>fighting against the Russians and the Germans</u>.
4. <u>Tallinn</u> is the <u>capital</u> of Estonia. It is also the <u>historic heart of Estonian history and culture</u>. The walls and gates of <u>the old city center</u> date back to the 13th century.
5. Estonians are very fond of <u>singing</u>. There are often <u>choral concerts</u> in the churches and concert halls and also many informal opportunities to hear <u>vocal music</u>.
6. Every year, a <u>national song contest</u> is held in Estonia. Singers from all over the country meet and sing in <u>the competition</u>. <u>This event</u> is shown on television and is very popular with young Estonians.
7. The <u>old city hall</u> stands in the main square in the center of Tallinn. <u>This beautiful medieval building</u> is no longer <u>the seat of the city government</u>. It is now used for special events.
8. The <u>University of Tartu</u> is in the smaller city of Tartu, to the southeast of Tallinn. Estonia's oldest and largest <u>educational institution</u>, it attracts students from many other countries. For this reason, many <u>courses</u> are held in English.
9. Many people who live in Tallinn also have <u>vacation homes</u> on the nearby island of Saaremaa in the Baltic Sea. These may be just <u>simple cottages</u>, but they are often surrounded by large gardens full of flowers, fruit trees, and vegetables.
10. Estonians love a good <u>cup of coffee</u>. In the center of Tallinn, there are many small coffee shops where they can enjoy <u>their favorite drink</u> and also chat with friends.

Exercise 8 *(page 103)*

1. The Rise of Factories

The first <u>factories</u> opened in the United States after 1815, and soon there were factories in all the major cities. <u>Industrialization</u> had direct consequences on the American (labor force) Before the factories, most <u>manufacturing</u> was done at home, where (people) had control over the way they worked, in particular their movements and their time. With factories, however, (workers) lost all control over their |jobs.| The new <u>methods of production</u> required a stricter sense of time. Work began at the sound of a bell and workers had to |keep machines operating all day.| They could not be late or absent, as that could interfere with <u>production</u>. Furthermore, in <u>the industrial system</u>, there was no room for (personal invention or creativity) Workers were not encouraged to (think for themselves) or to take pride in the products, but simply to |follow instructions| —and above all, |keep production moving.| In this way, industrialization not only made a difference in the way work was organized; it completely changed |the nature of work.|

2. Workers' Reactions to Industrialization

The first workers to arrive in the factories <u>had trouble</u> (getting used to) the |new methods of production.| They <u>did not have an easy time</u>, first of all, (adapting to) the strict |schedule.| Some of them began to hate the sound of the bell that signaled the beginning of their |working day.| It came to represent their loss of freedom. Furthermore, the <u>conditions</u>

in the factories were terrible by modern standards. The workers had to <u>work quickly</u> to keep up with the machines, which meant repeating the same movements rapidly all day. Factory days were also very long—10 or even 12 hours a day, six days a week. And finally, the machines were noisy, dirty, and dangerous, often injuring or killing the people working with them. It is not surprising that a certain number of workers <u>could not cope with</u> the situation and left the factories. Others looked for ways to protect themselves and formed the first unions.

PART 3 COMPREHENSION SKILLS

UNIT 1
Scanning and Previewing

Exercises 1-5: The answers to these exercises can all be found by looking back at the scanned text.

Exercises 6-10: Answers will vary.

FOV
Unit 1

Exercise 1 (page 125)

D. 1. T   2. F   3. F   4. T   5. T

Exercise 2 (page 126)

1. b   5. c
2. c   6. b
3. a   7. a
4. a   8. c

Exercise 3 (page 128)

1. break   5. job
2. interesting   6. at least
3. several   7. make
4. have   8. property

Exercise 4 (page 128)

1. charged with   5. branch
2. operation   6. massive
3. struck   7. statement
4. currently   8. carrying out

Exercise 5 (page 129)

1. extend   5. branch
2. acquire   6. charge with
3. significant   7. estimate
4. carry out   8. exceed

Exercise 6 (page 130)

	Noun	Verb	Adjective	Negative Adjective	Adverb
1.	acquisition	acquire	acquisitive, acquiring	X	X
2.	estimation, estimate	estimate	estimated	X	X
3.	excess	exceed	excessive	X	excessively
4.	extension, extent	extend	extensive, extended	X	extensively
5.	finances	finance	financial	X	financially
6.	operation, operator	operate	operational	nonoperational	operationally
7.	significance	signify	significant	insignificant	significantly
8.	statement	state	stated, stately	unstated	X
9.	strike	strike	striking	X	strikingly

(Other inferences may be possible.)

Exercise 1 *(page 132)*

1. Outside a theater or concert hall
2. Waiting for someone to come out of the theater
3. Probably an actor or a musician
4. He or she is a little embarrassed and impatient. He or she doesn't care so much about the actor/musician.
5. He or she is a real fan of the actor/musician.
6. Answers will vary.

Exercise 2 *(page 133)*

1. In a store
2. Looking for a present for someone, probably something small like jewelry (it fits in his pocket)
3. Probably B's wife
4. A is a salesperson in a store, probably a woman, since this seems to be the women's part of the store and that is usually an area where women work. She could be any age. She's very patient.
5. B is probably a man. He needs to buy a birthday or holiday present for his wife or partner. He's probably not young, as it seems they have been married or living together for a while. Also, the salesperson suggests that the person receiving the present is not a young woman.
6. Answers will vary.

Exercise 3 *(page 134)*

1. In a pub, bar, or restaurant
2. Flora is married to someone else and they are meeting secretly, as they have been for some time.
3. A group of people who are friends and who are talking and having fun
4. Probably her husband's
5. Answers will vary.

Exercise 4 *(page 135)*

1. They are walking down a city street in an area with expensive shops.
2. They are good friends, maybe also colleagues, and they spend quite of lot of time together.
3. They are almost afraid of the wealth and luxury, and of the doorman and the clerk, so to cover their fear, they pretend to be superior.
4. The clerk feels superior to them because he can see that they can't afford any of the jewelry in the store. He behaves in an overly polite manner toward them.
5. This story probably takes place some time ago in the 20th century when having a mink coat was seen as the mark of a rich and successful woman.
6. Answers will vary.

Exercise 5 *(page 137)*

1. truck driver
2. mailman/woman
3. car salesman

Exercise 6 (page 138)

1. f. newspaper article
2. d. letter from a nonprofit organization
3. e. e-mail message from a bank
4. a. product information on a package
5. b. encyclopedia article

Exercise 7 (page 139)

1. a. Since snakes are predators (they eat other animals), their decline might mean an increase in population for the animals they usually eat.
   b. The text says that snakes are "vital" predators. That means they are necessary. Without them, there might be many more mice or similar animals that eat rice and other kinds of grain.
   c. The wider consequences for some animals, such as mice, might be positive, since fewer snakes will mean fewer mice eaten by snakes. It might also be positive for other animals that eat mice, such as cats or foxes. For farmers, it will probably be negative, since more mice will eat more of their rice or other crops.
2. a. Santino made piles of rocks so he could throw them at people visiting the zoo.
   b. Because he was aggressive and seemed angry at other animals and people.
   c. They didn't think that chimpanzees were capable of planning ahead, but when Santino hid rocks to throw or when he broke off pieces of cement, he showed he could think about what he would do in the future.

Exercise 8 (page 140)

1. seals, penguins, flightless birds, and maybe other birds
2. to hunt seals and penguins for meat, fur, and oil
3. It affected them indirectly: The disease killed many rabbits, so the cats had fewer rabbits to eat, and they started hunting birds. This led to the extinction of two more kinds of birds.
4. They could have caused it in two ways: by eating all the vegetation so that the soil eroded, and by digging lots of holes, which might have loosened the soil.
5. They may be afraid that the cats will start hunting the birds again. Or they may be referring to consequences that haven't yet been imagined.

FOV
Unit 2

Exercise 1 (page 141)

D. 1. F   2. T   3. F   4. T   5. T

Exercise 2 (page 143)

1. d   2. g   3. f   4. a   5. h   6. b   7. i   8. c

Exercise 3 (page 143)

1. history
2. fortunately
3. choose
4. bring together
5. idea
6. belief
7. learn
8. review

Exercise 4 (page 144)

1. issues
2. unemployment
3. myth
4. building up
5. rating
6. revealed
7. apparently
8. recommend

Exercise 5 *(page 144)*

1. reveal	3. effective	5. adopt	7. emerge
2. joint	4. vast	6. build up	8. issue

Exercise 6 *(page 145)*

	Noun	Verb	Adjective	Negative Adjective	Adverb
1.	adoption	adopt	adoptive	X	X
2.	awareness	X	aware	unaware	X
3.	concern	concern	concerned	unconcerned	X
4.	effect	effect	effective	ineffective	effectively
5.	emergence	emerge	emerging	X	X
6.	employment, unemployment	employ	employable	unemployable	X
7.	joint	join	joint	X	jointly
8.	myth	X	mythical	X	X
9.	presence, presentation	present	present	X	presently
10.	rating	rate	rated	unrated	X
11.	revelation	reveal	revealing	unrevealing	X
12.	recommendation	recommend	recommended	X	X
13.	vastness	X	vast	X	vastly

UNIT 3
Understanding Paragraphs

(The wording of ideas may vary.)

Exercise 1 *(page 148)*

1. foods made from milk; ice cream
2. parts of a tree; leaves
3. types of books; fiction
4. parts of a car; steering wheel
5. geometric shapes; square
6. Canadian cities; Montreal
7. kitchen appliances; refrigerator
8. ways of moving forward; run
9. things/people in a restaurant; menu
10. tropical fruits; banana
11. kinds of metal; iron
12. geographical features; hills

Exercise 2 *(page 149)*

1. farm animals that are kept for meat; mice
2. kinds of insects; pigeon
3. ways of cooking food; stir
4. joints in the body; rib
5. buildings people live in; apartment
6. world religions; Nationalism
7. green vegetables; potatoes
8. things found at the beach; bicycle
9. jobs traditionally done by women; mechanic
10. mathematical operations; review
11. things for drinking from; jar
12. organs in the body; spine

Exercise 3 *(page 150)*

Topic: doing the laundry

Exercise 4 *(page 153)*

A. 1. a   2. c   3. c

B. 1.

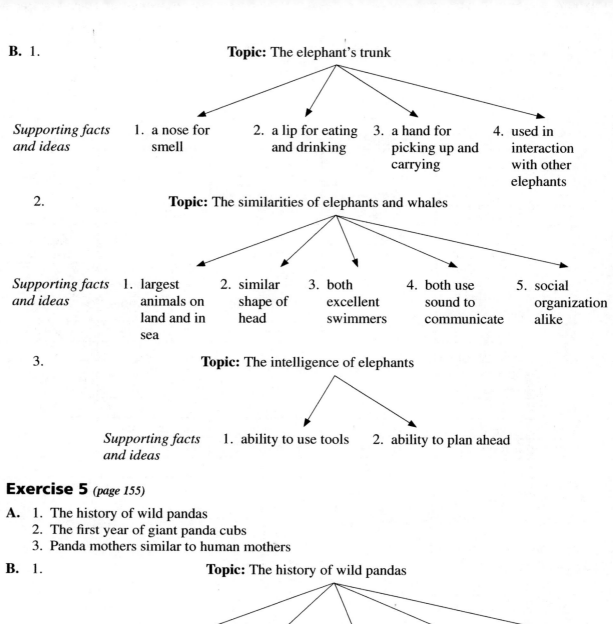

Topic: The elephant's trunk

Supporting facts and ideas

1. a nose for smell
2. a lip for eating and drinking
3. a hand for picking up and carrying
4. used in interaction with other elephants

2.

Topic: The similarities of elephants and whales

Supporting facts and ideas

1. largest animals on land and in sea
2. similar shape of head
3. both excellent swimmers
4. both use sound to communicate
5. social organization alike

3.

Topic: The intelligence of elephants

Supporting facts and ideas

1. ability to use tools
2. ability to plan ahead

Exercise 5 *(page 155)*

A. 1. The history of wild pandas
2. The first year of giant panda cubs
3. Panda mothers similar to human mothers

B. 1.

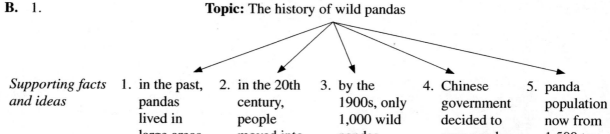

Topic: The history of wild pandas

Supporting facts and ideas

1. in the past, pandas lived in large areas of China
2. in the 20th century, people moved into forests
3. by the 1900s, only 1,000 wild pandas
4. Chinese government decided to save pandas
5. panda population now from 1,500 to 2,000

2.

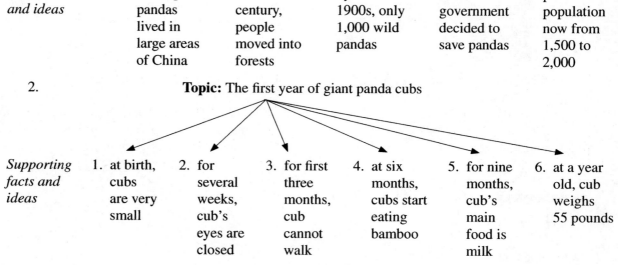

Topic: The first year of giant panda cubs

Supporting facts and ideas

1. at birth, cubs are very small
2. for several weeks, cub's eyes are closed
3. for first three months, cub cannot walk
4. at six months, cubs start eating bamboo
5. for nine months, cub's main food is milk
6. at a year old, cub weighs 55 pounds

3. **Topic:** Panda mothers similar to human mothers in some ways

Supporting facts and ideas
1. keep their babies very clean
2. hold their babies in front paws
3. rock their babies when they cry
4. take care of their babies for quite a while

Exercise 6 *(page 157)*

A. 1. b   2. c   3. b

Exercise 7 *(page 159)*

B. 1. **Main Idea:** When people draw maps of the world, they make all kinds of mistakes.

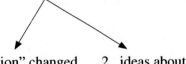

Supporting facts and ideas
1. many people have difficulty drawing
2. people don't know the size of the continents
3. everyone makes Europe too large and Africa too small

2. **Main Idea:** There are several reasons why people imagine Europe larger and Africa smaller than they are.

Supporting facts and ideas
1. "Mercator projection" changed sizes of areas on maps
2. ideas about size influenced by ideas about importance

3. **Main Idea:** Maps of Africa contained errors until people explored it better and discovered the errors.

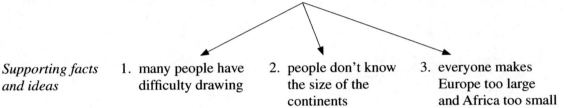

Supporting facts and ideas
1. in 1790s, an explorer reported mountains in Africa
2. in 1798, a map of Africa called them the Kong Mountains
3. Kong Mountains were on maps of Africa for 100 years
4. in 1887, an explorer found these mountains did not exist

Exercise 8 *(page 161)*

1. d   2. a   3. c   4. b   5. c

Exercise 9 *(page 162)*

1. a   2. c   3. b   4. c   5. d

Exercise 10 *(page 163)*

1. b   2. a   3. d   4. c   5. b

Exercise 11 *(page 164)*

1. d   2. b   3. a   4. b   5. c

Exercise 1 *(page 166)*

D. 1. F   2. F   3. T   4. T   5. T

Exercise 2 *(page 168)*

1. b   2. a   3. a   4. c   5. b   6. c   7. a   8. b

Exercise 3 *(page 169)*

1. b   2. e   3. g   4. h   5. i   6. a   7. c   8. f

Exercise 4 *(page 169)*

1. g   2. e   3. f   4. h   5. b   6. d   7. a   8. c

Exercise 5 *(page 170)*

1. conflict
2. avoid
3. affect
4. balance
5. vehicles
6. ahead
7. reaction

Exercise 6 *(page 171)*

	Noun	Verb	Adjective	Negative Adjective	Adverb
1.	avoidance	avoid	avoidable	unavoidable	X
2.	balance	balance	balanced	unbalanced	X
3.	conflict	conflict	conflicting, conflicted	X	X
4.	consideration	consider	considerable, considerate	inconsiderate	considerably, considerately
5.	location, locale, locality	locate	local	X	locally
6.	measure, measurement	measure	measurable	immeasurable	measurably
7.	occurrence	occur	X	X	X
8.	reaction	react	reactive	X	X
9.	recovery	recover	recoverable	unrecoverable	X
10.	sense, sensitivity	sense, sensitize	sensitive	insensitive	sensitively
11.	solidity, solid	solidify	solid	X	solidly

(The wording of ideas may vary.)

Exercise 2 *(page 174)*

1. 1. Main idea: Where rich people see trash, poor people see all kinds of opportunities.
2. Listing pattern signal words: all kinds of
3. Supporting facts and ideas:

1. in U.S., some people make a living from trash	2. in American and European cities, homeless people look for food and clothes in trash cans	3. in developing countries, people collect trash in garbage dumps and sell it

4. Signal words/phrases: some, also, for example

2. 1. Main idea: The computers thrown away in the U.S. come to an end in various ways.
2. Listing pattern signal word: various
3. Supporting facts and ideas:

1. millions of computers thrown into trash, end up in dumps	2. some computers brought to recycling centers	3. specialized companies take some computers apart and reuse parts	4. some computers sent to developing countries

4. Signal words/phrases: A certain number, Other, Sometimes, Other

3. 1. Main idea: Since people arrived in Antarctica they have dealt with the trash in a number of ways.
2. Listing pattern signal word/phrase: a number of
3. Supporting facts and ideas:

1. in early years things left where they were	2. some visitors put trash in hole in the ground	3. most now take trash home	4. some dump trash into the ocean

4. Signal words/phrases: many, Some, Most, a certain number of

Exercise 3 *(page 177)*

1. 1. Main idea: Jackie Robinson was born in Georgia and then moved to California.
2. Sequence pattern signal word: born
3. Supporting facts and ideas:

1. born in 1919	2. family moved to California	3. older brother became track star	4. in high school most valuable player	5. at U.C. played four sports	6. left U.C. in 1941

4. Signal words/phrases: in 1919, After his father left the family, in the 1936 Olympics, in high school, at U.C., in 1941

2. 1. Main idea: Robinson had difficulties in the U.S. because of racial discrimination.
  2. Sequence pattern signal words: In 1942
  3. Supporting facts and ideas:

1. joined the U.S. Army	2. blacks separate from whites on buses	3. R. refused to move to back of army bus	4. R. was arrested	5. army recognized R. was right	6. war was almost over

  4. Signal words/phrases: In 1942, At that time, one day, When, Eventually, By that time

3. 1. Main idea: Robinson's baseball career began in 1946 and ended in 1956.
  2. Sequence pattern signal words: began in 1946
  3. Supporting facts and ideas:

1. career began with Montreal Royals	2. had trouble because he was the only black player	3. moved to major leagues— Brooklyn Dodgers	4. awarded prize for best young player	5. Dodger's most valuable player

  4. Signal words/phrases: in 1946, in the beginning, The next year, After his first year, From then until his retirement in 1956

Exercise 4 *(page 178)*

1. 1. Main idea: When you are going to give a book talk, you need to prepare it carefully.
  2. Sequence pattern signal words: When, you need to prepare it
  3. Supporting facts and ideas:

1. choose a book	2. make notes	3. practice talking from notes	4. time yourself	5. practice talk with a friend or record it

  4. Signal words/phrases: First, After you have decided, Then, At this point, Finally

2. 1. Main idea: To make a good meat broth, you need to have good ingredients.
  2. Sequence pattern signal words: To make, you need to have
  3. Supporting facts and ideas:

1. buy several kinds of meat	2. put meat in large pot and add water	3. add carrots, celery, and parsley	4. put broth on stove	5. turn heat down and let it cook

  4. Signal words/phrases: First, The next step, Then, At this point, Now, When it is boiling

Exercise 5 *(page 180)*

1. 1. Main idea: Italian universities are quite different from most American universities.
   2. Comparison pattern signal words: quite different from
   3. Supporting facts and ideas:

   1. setting in U.S. is campus; setting in Italy is city
   2. American universities have green space; Italian universities do not
   3. American students live in dorms; Italian students live at home or in apartments

   4. Signal words/phrases: One difference, However, while, Another important difference, on the other hand

2. 1. Main idea: In both Italian and American universities, a certain percentage of students start but never graduate.
   2. Comparison pattern signal word: both
   3. Supporting facts and ideas:

   1. students cannot afford to pay
   2. students make poor choices about courses
   3. students have psychological problems

   4. Signal words/phrases: In some cases, both, even though, both

3. 1. Main idea: University programs in Italy and the U.S. are organized in different ways.
   2. Comparison pattern signal word: different
   3. Supporting facts and ideas:

   1. universities in both countries have course requirements
   2. in Italy, students' courses in chosen field
   3. in U.S., students take courses outside major
   4. Italian students not required to attend classes
   5. American students required to attend classes

   4. Signal words/phrases: both, however, on the other hand, one big difference, Instead, however

Exercise 6 *(page 183)*

1. 1. Main idea: Traveling from one city or country to another can contribute to the spread of disease.
   2. Cause/effect pattern signal word: can contribute to
   3. Supporting facts and ideas:

   1. travelers arrive in new place with germs
   2. people have no protection, so catch disease
   3. disease not identified, so no measures taken
   4. disease spreads through population

   4. Signal words/phrases: so, because, In this way,

2. 1. Main idea: Heating and cooling systems can be a source of disease.
　2. Cause/effect pattern signal words: can be a source of
　3. Supporting facts and ideas:

　　1. air conditioners are a common source of health problems (germs grow in them and are blown into homes and offices)

　　2. heating/cooling systems of large buildings can also cause illness (germs grow in cooling towers and are sent through buildings with air conditioning)

　4. Signal words/phrases: are cause of, creates, make, can cause, arise, affect

3. 1. Main idea: Pollution of the oceans can also be a factor in spreading disease.
　2. Cause/effect pattern signal words: be a factor
　3. Supporting facts and ideas:

　　1. pollution caused by chemicals or human waste

　　2. pollutants result in algae growth, habitat for cholera

　　3. algae and cholera stick to ship bottoms and travel around world

　4. Signal words/phrases: be caused by, result in, causing

Exercise 7 *(page 185)*

1. 1. Main idea: A new invention can be used to help keep food fresh in hot weather without using electricity.
　2. Problem-solution signal words: no way to keep food fresh (problem); invented/a new kind of cooler (solution)
　3. Supporting facts and ideas:

　　1. many people in developing countries don't have electricity, so they can't keep food fresh in hot weather

　　2. a new kind of cooler is made of two clay pots with wet sand and wet cloth

　　3. useful for developing countries since easy, inexpensive, doesn't require ice or electricity

　4. Signal words/phrases: various signal words/phrases for other patterns

2. 1. Main idea: Scientists and inventors are working hard to develop stoves that will be more efficient, safer, and less polluting.
　2. Problem-solution signal words: pollution and illness (problem); working to develop (solution)
　3. Supporting facts and ideas:

　　1. cooking stoves produce a lot of smoke and gases

　　2. gases kill many people directly and indirectly

　　3. gases contribute to global warming

　　4. scientists and inventors working to develop better stove

　4. Signal words/phrases: various signal words/phrases for other patterns

3. 1. Main idea: *The Weza* makes it possible for many Africans with cell phones to recharge them.
   2. Problem-solution signal words: need to be recharged (problem); invention/helpful in this situation (solution)
   3. Supporting facts and ideas:

1. cell phone use in Africa has expanded recently	2. batteries need to be recharged	3. many Africans have no access to electricity	4. *Weza* foot pump produces electric power to charge phones

   4. Signal words/phrases: various signal words/phrases for other patterns

Exercise 8 *(page 187)*

1. Sequence
2. Listing
3. Problem-solution
4. Cause/effect
5. Comparison

Exercise 9 *(page 188)*

1. a. Sequence
   b. Sequence
   c. Comparison

2. a. Listing (Description)
   b. Comparison
   c. Listing

3. a. Listing
   b. Cause/effect
   c. Sequence

FOV
Unit 4

Exercise 1 *(page 189)*

D. 1. T   2. T   3. F   4. F   5. F

Exercise 2 *(page 191)*

1. c   2. a   3. f   4. g   5. d   6. i   7. e   8. b

Exercise 3 *(page 191)*

1. be regarded as   5. assume
2. impression   6. actually
3. appearance   7. overcome
4. tend   8. involved

Exercise 4 *(page 192)*

1. meet   5. registered as
2. now   6. expensive
3. inform   7. unhappy
4. application   8. open to

Exercise 5 (page 192)

1. overcome	3. complex	5. access	7. intention
2. analyze	4. intense	6. impression	

Exercise 6 (page 193)

	Noun	Verb	Adjective	Negative Adjective	Adverb
1.	access, accessibility	access	accessible	inaccessible	X
2.	actuality	actualize	actual	X	actually
3.	analysis	analyze	analytical	X	analytically
4.	appearance	appear	apparent	X	apparently
5.	assumption	assume	X	X	X
6.	complexity	X	complex	X	complexly
7.	impression	impress	impressive	unimpressive	impressively
8.	intensity	intensify	intense	X	intensely
9.	intention	intend	intentional, intended	unintentional, unintended	intentionally, unintentionally
10.	involvement	involve	involving, involved	uninvolved	X
11.	limitation, limit	limit	limited	unlimited	X
12.	tendency	tend	X	X	X

UNIT 5
Reading Longer Passages

(The wording and selection of ideas may vary.)

Exercise 1 (page 198)

A. Overall idea: A cyclist who was hit by the patrol car of police officer Louis Ramos has brought charges against him for driving away without reporting the accident.
B. Overall pattern: Sequence
C. Supporting facts and ideas:
   1. Officer Ramos was driving the wrong way on a one-way street; drove through a red light
   2. Ramos and partner got out of car, pulled the cyclist over to the sidewalk, drove off without reporting the accident or calling an ambulance
   3. The cyclist suffered cuts and bruises, a broken nose and wrist.
   4. Ramos pleaded not guilty; he and Anderson suspended without pay.

Exercise 2 (page 199)

   1. A. Overall idea: The three children who were lost all last night were found this icy morning.
      B. Overall pattern: Problem-solution, sequence
      C. Supporting facts and ideas:
         1. The children spent night in swamp
         2. Rescuers out all night searching in the swamp; George Hammond brought back the children
         3. An ambulance brought them to Plymouth Hospital; minor injuries, in good condition
         4. Police had high-tech equipment, but common sense led to children.
         5. The children said they were very afraid at times.

2. A. Overall idea: Police carried out one of the biggest operations ever against the 'Ndrangheta, currently one of the most powerful Italian crime organizations.
   B. Overall pattern: Problem-solution
   C. Supporting facts and ideas:
      1. Among those arrested: the organization's boss of bosses, the leader of the Milan branch, local government officials
      2. Those arrested are charged with criminal association, murder, arms, and drug trafficking.
      3. 'Ndrangheta, based in Calabria, property and political influence in north of Italy, increasing wealth from drugs from South America
      4. 'Ndrangheta reach far beyond Italy's borders, in Australia and Canada
      5. Operation struck significant blow to leadership and finances
      6. Revenue of Italy's main crime groups is 135 billion euros = 9 percent of Italy's gross domestic product

Exercise 3 *(page 201)*

A. Overall idea: France has for centuries had a reputation for culinary excellence and Britain for some of the worst cooking in the world. But according to a recent poll, that reputation may no longer reflect reality.
B. Overall pattern: Comparison
C. Supporting facts and ideas:
   1. Results of poll suggest British spend more time cooking and produce greater variety of dishes than French.
   2. Reaction in London enthusiastic. Lulu Grimes: British food greatly improved, home cooks range of ingredients, preparing new dishes; Marilyn Jarmon: improvement in British food, eats well in London, greater diversity now
   3. Some French say survey is not the whole picture. Jeannine Loiret: French women cook less during the week but more on weekends; Jean-Paul Belmonde: people in Paris don't cook much, but elsewhere cooking is still important at the heart of daily life; Bernard Blier: British food is not very refined. I'm not a fan at all.

Exercise 4 *(page 202)*

1. A. Overall idea: Ninety percent of the human race is affected by motion sickness of one kind or another.
   B. Overall pattern: Problem-solution
   C. Supporting facts and ideas:
      1. Motion sickness when the brain cannot make sense of the messages, so sends signals to stomach that something wrong
      2. Preventative measures: eat lightly before a trip, snack often on plain foods, avoid alcoholic and carbonated drinks, high-fat foods, and spices.
      3. Location of seat is important; plane—sit near the wings; car—sit in the front seat and keep the windows open; boat—stay outside or at the front and look ahead
      4. People can take various medications.
      5. Take measures even if you've never had motion sickness before.

2. A. Overall idea: Online dating has gone mainstream and academics are analyzing it.
    B. Overall pattern: Part problem-solution, part comparison
    C. Supporting facts and ideas:
        1. Dr. Jeff Gavin researched how we talk and relate to people through computers and the Internet.
        2. People found ways to overcome limitations of online communication by noticing other cues.
        3. Gavin compared members of UK and Japanese online dating sites: the Japanese more indirect with body language, silence, social cues; Western communication depends more on content.
        4. Japanese online daters overcome lack of social information by developing their own cues.
        5. Japanese use Internet differently than British; access it more from mobile phones.
        6. Bad situations used to happen with people lying about their appearance, but that happens less now.
        7. People make improvements to their profiles, but that's normal like before going out at night.

Exercise 5 *(page 203)*

A. Overall idea: The homeless are among the extremely poor.
B. Overall pattern: Cause/effect, comparison (and Definition)
C. Supporting facts and ideas:
    1. Peter Rossi's study: Most are African American men in mid-30s. Other studies: women and families with children, alcohol and drug abusers, people who are mentally ill
    2. The homeless today differ in some ways from the homeless of the 1950s and 1960s: more families; more visible because more likely to sleep on the streets
    3. Homelessness today the result of at least three social forces: (1) less inexpensive housing; (2) less demand for unskilled labor; (3) government has cut back on public welfare benefits

Exercise 6 *(page 204)*

A. Overall idea: The law of demand says that when the price of something is lower, consumers will buy more of it. When the price is higher, consumers will buy less of it.
B. Overall pattern: Cause/effect (or Definition)
C. Supporting facts and ideas:
    1. The price of something will strongly influence your decision to buy it.
    2. The law of demand is not the result of one pattern of behavior, but of two separate patterns that overlap
    3. The Substitution Effect: A consumer reacts to a rise in the price of one good by consuming less of that good and more of a substitute good.
    4. The Income Effect: Rising prices make us feel poorer so we buy less; lower prices make us feel wealthier, so we buy more.

FOV
Unit 5

Exercise 1 *(page 205)*

  1. F   2. F   3. T   4. T   5. T

Exercise 2 *(page 207)*

  1. c   2. a   3. b   4. b   5. c   6. a   7. c   8. b

Exercise 3 *(page 208)*

  1. d   2. e   3. a   4. h   5. g   6. i   7. f   8. b

Exercise 4 (page 209)

1. trade
2. provide
3. practical
4. specialized
5. serve as
6. in terms of

Exercise 5 (page 209)

1. practical
2. specialized
3. experience
4. means
5. provide
6. determine

Exercise 6 (page 210)

	Noun	Verb	Adjective	Negative Adjective	Adverb
1.	appreciation	appreciate	appreciative	unappreciative	X
2.	determination	determine	determined	undetermined	X
3.	exception	X	exceptional	unexceptional	exceptionally
4.	function	function	functional	dysfunctional	functionally
5.	practice, practicality	practice	practical	impractical	practically
6.	provision, provider	provide	provisional	X	provisionally
7.	service, servant, serving	serve	serviceable	unserviceable	X
8.	specialty, specialization	specialize	specialized	X	specially
9.	will, willingness	will	willing	unwilling	willingly

Unit 6
Skimming

(Answers to all exercises will vary.)

FOV
Unit 6

Exercise 1 (page 222)

D. 1. F   2. T   3. T   4. F   5. T

Exercise 2 (page 224)

1. d   2. e   3. g   4. i   5. c   6. f   7. a   8. b

Exercise 3 (page 224)

1. accident
2. drive
3. chance
4. make up
5. different
6. order from
7. widely
8. feel

Exercise 4 (page 225)

1. damage
2. process
3. ranging from
4. injury
5. pressure
6. release
7. relief
8. substance

Exercise 5 (page 225)

1. essential
2. release
3. potential
4. process
5. injury
6. damage
7. substance
8. relief

Exercise 6 (page 226)

	Noun	Verb	Adjective	Negative Adjective	Adverb
1.	damage	damage	damaging, damaged	undamaged	X
2.	domination, dominance	dominate	dominating	X	X
3.	essence	X	essential	unessential	essentially
4.	harm	harm	harmful	harmless	harmlessly
5.	injury	injure	injured	uninjured	X
6.	sense, sensation, sensitivity	sense	sensitive, sensible	insensitive, senseless	sensitively, senselessly, sensibly
7.	lead, leader	lead	leading	X	X
8.	potential	potentialize	potential	X	potentially
9.	process	process	processed	unprocessed	X
10.	range	range	X	X	X
11.	relief	relieve	relieved	unrelieved	X
12.	substance	substantiate	substantial	insubstantial	substantially

Harry Houdini: The Life of an Escape Artist

Exercise 1 (page 237)

C. 1. c   5. b
2. a   6. a
3. a   7. b
4. b   8. c

Exercise 2 (page 239)

C. 1. a   5. b
2. c   6. c
3. b   7. c
4. c   8. b

Exercise 3 (page 241)

C. 1. b   5. c
2. c   6. c
3. b   7. a
4. c   8. b

Exercise 4 (page 243)

C. 1. c   5. c
2. c   6. a
3. a   7. b
4. b   8. a

Exercise 5 (page 245)

C. 1. c   5. b
2. c   6. a
3. a   7. b
4. c   8. c

Exercise 6 (page 247)

C. 1. a   5. b
2. c   6. c
3. c   7. c
4. a   8. a

Exercise 7 (page 249)

C. 1. b   5. a
2. a   6. c
3. a   7. b
4. c   8. a

Exercise 8 (page 251)

C. 1. c   5. b
2. b   6. b
3. b   7. b
4. b   8. c

Making a Living

Exercise 1 (page 253)

C. 1. b   5. a
2. c   6. c
3. a   7. b
4. c   8. a

Exercise 2 (page 255)

C. 1. a   5. a
2. c   6. b
3. a   7. b
4. b   8. a

Exercise 3 (page 257)

C. 1. c   5. c
2. a   6. b
3. b   7. a
4. a   8. c

Exercise 4 (page 259)

C. 1. a   5. a
2. a   6. c
3. c   7. b
4. a   8. a

Exercise 5 (page 261)

C. 1. c   5. c
2. b   6. a
3. c   7. c
4. a   8. b

Exercise 6 (page 263)

C. 1. b   5. a
2. c   6. a
3. b   7. a
4. c   8. c

Exercise 7 (page 265)

C. 1. a   5. b
2. c   6. a
3. a   7. c
4. a   8. c

Exercise 8 (page 267)

C. 1. c   5. b
    2. a   6. b
    3. a   7. a
    4. c   8. a

UNIT 3
Better Lives in a Better World

Exercise 1 (page 269)

C. 1. b   5. c
    2. c   6. a
    3. b   7. a
    4. c   8. b

Exercise 2 (page 271)

C. 1. c   5. b
    2. a   6. a
    3. a   7. b
    4. c   8. a

Exercise 3 (page 273)

C. 1. a   5. b
    2. c   6. c
    3. a   7. b
    4. c   8. b

Exercise 4 (page 275)

C. 1. b   5. c
    2. b   6. b
    3. b   7. c
    4. a   8. c

Exercise 5 (page 277)

C. 1. b   5. c
    2. a   6. b
    3. c   7. c
    4. c   8. a

Exercise 6 (page 279)

C. 1. a   5. c
    2. c   6. a
    3. a   7. b
    4. b   8. c

Exercise 7 (page 281)

C. 1. a   5. a
    2. b   6. a
    3. c   7. c
    4. c   8. b

Exercise 8 (page 283)

C. 1. c   5. b
    2. a   6. a
    3. a   7. b
    4. c   8. c